Unusual Aberdonians: 36 (ish) Lives Less Ordinary in the North East of Scotland

LIA SANDERS

In memory of Anne Doogan and Patrick Slater, two lives less ordinary.

CONTENTS

INTRODUCTION

Aberdeen is not very good at celebrating its history. Although we have stories that rival those told in Edinburgh or London, we seldom talk about them, except among local history enthusiasts. But the situation is worse than that – not only do we not talk about our history, many of us do not know much about it either.

Of course, the information is out there, if you choose to go looking for it. But there is something about the minutiae of local history that causes the casual investigator to start snoring lightly as their eyelids droop. Much of it is only of interest if you yourself have walked those streets, knew those shops, remember those legends. Where nostalgia begins to blur together with history, it ceases to have mass appeal.

And that is a shame. Because I believe that Aberdeen's history has the potential to enthral, to engage even those people who know nothing about the city and are only here for a brief stopover on the way from Edinburgh to Inverness. Over the last three years, this is something that my tour business, Scot Free Tours, has successfully proven, beguiling visitors from Cardiff to Costa Rica, from Singapore to Sweden, who are often moved to remark that they had no idea that Aberdeen was so interesting.

Anywhere can be interesting, of course, as long as it has people. We humans are endlessly fascinating to one another, particular those of us who seem to flout convention or who get mixed up in something far greater than themselves.

But maybe Aberdeenshire has been particularly blessed with eccentrics, rogues, fly-by-nighters, chancers, victims of circumstance, happy-go-luckys, forces-of-nature and unique specimens of humanity. This book is all about such people, individuals who may – or may not – have achieved great things, but whose primary claim to inclusion is that their stories are stranger than fiction, whether through unconventional behaviour or the ways that others treated them.

I cannot claim to much original research; I am standing on the shoulders of others. My aim is that instead of you, the reader, having to wade through 200-odd books and articles on these individuals, I have done the digging for you. Think of this as your primer to the 'characters' of the North East of Scotland, with only the choicest facts included. And perhaps, if one person catches your imagination, you can investigate them further yourself.

This does mean that I have generally been limited to those figures whom others have already researched. Although I have gestured at diversity of gender, class and – to a lesser extent – sexuality, this book is predominantly made up of white people. It would be thought-provoking to get a perspective on the experiences of James Burnett's[1] African servant Gory, living in 18th century Aberdeenshire and Edinburgh, to discover more about the time some of the Satsuma Nineteen[2] studied in Aberdeen, or to learn about what it was like to be Nathaniel Thomas King, the first African graduate from the University of Aberdeen, who graduated in Medicine in 1874, becoming the first Nigerian to achieve medical qualifications. However, if the sources are out there, I have not been able to find them. I hope that in the future someone will take on the necessary work.

But although restricted by the research of others, the people included are here entirely by my own whim. Some have earned their place by virtue of being born in Aberdeenshire, brought up here or dying here. Some spent formative years here or had important experiences here. Some were just too good to leave out. Each of them is someone that I, personally, find fascinating. I hope you will too. And I hope you will enjoy learning a little bit more about the people of Aberdeenshire and passing those stories

---

[1] See 5. James Burnett, Lord Monboddo.
[2] Read about them in 3. Thomas Blake Glover.

on. The trouble with tours is that they are ephemeral. With this book, you will be able to remember some of these often-forgotten individuals.

Lia Sanders, 14.05.2019

Handling Guide

This is not a bedside table book, for you to read each entry in alphabetical order, night after night. It is what I would describe as a loo book, something for you to dip into at random and peruse an entry or two while on the bog. If you want to know what you are getting into, there is a thematic contents at the back, telling you what category each person belongs to, from hardened criminals to acclaimed doctors.

1. JOHN HENRY ANDERSON

Magician Willing to Die for his Tricks

1814 - 1874

In Aberdeen's St Nicholas Kirkyard, there is a small, rather humble, white gravestone tucked away off the main path. This was all that John Henry Anderson could afford to honour his mother, whose death left him in charge of his six younger siblings. He was just 16 years old.

Fast forward 79 years and the grave had an internationally renowned visitor: Harry Houdini. The famous illusionist visited the Granite City in June 1909 and had his photograph taken beside the headstone. He was appalled at the condition of the grave and plot and paid for it to be restored.

Why was Houdini so interested in this grave? In 1874, John was buried in the same plot as his mother. Houdini was a great admirer of the man known professionally as 'The Great Wizard of the North' but their paths were never to cross. Houdini was born 49 days after John died – it speaks to the latter's importance, both as a magician and as a self-promoter, that 35 years later Houdini would seek out his final resting place.

At the time of his mother's death, John had already been working as a call boy and bit-part actor in a travelling theatre company for two years. This first exposed him to the world of magic and illusion and the following year he struck out on his own. When he was 25 years old, he met and performed for celebrated writer Sir Walter Scott. As the young magician was leaving, Scott said to him: 'They call me the Wizard of the North, but they are wrong; that title rightfully belongs to you.' John was so pleased with this compliment that he adopted the name 'The Great Wizard of the North' as his stage name and had the title engraved onto his umbrella handle.

This umbrella sometimes got him into difficulty. During the early stages of his career, he performed across Scotland and Ireland, regularly staying in small and superstitious villages. When the residents saw this engraving, they would wonder whether John was an agent of the devil. Often this worked out to his advantage as people would turn up to his shows in order to decide for themselves.

Although John was considered an excellent illusionist by those who saw him perform, it may be his talent for self-promotion that really set him apart. By the age of 31, Professor Anderson – as he was often known – had made enough money to build his own theatre in Glasgow. During his career, he performed across the globe, including in America, Australia and Russia. When in Russia, he committed the great faux pas of acknowledging the Tsar at a party. John feared that he was going to be sent to Siberia for this breach in etiquette; instead, Tsar Nicholas I sent for him to do a private performance. The Tsar admitted to John that he had been something of an amateur magician in his younger days and even taught his visitor a new trick.

It was one of many occasions when John performed to royalty. He also impressed the kings of Prussia, Sweden, Denmark and Hawaii. In 1849, he was a highlight of the 30th-birthday celebrations for Prince Albert, husband of Britain's Queen Victoria. His show for the Royal family at Balmoral Castle involved his inexhaustible bottle trick, where from the same, seemingly empty bottle he poured out whisky – and then proceeded to pour out any drink that the audience asked for, with sherry, milk, champagne and wine all coming from the same bottle. John concluded the trick by breaking the bottle and two white doves flew out.

At the time when John was performing, spiritualism was becoming popular. He used his fame and knowledge of magic to campaign against mediums who tricked the public into believing they were communicating with the spirit world. After having exposed the Davenport brothers – a pair of magicians who claimed their illusions were supernatural – in the United States, he returned to Britain. Back in his homeland, he would put on shows which would focus on conventional magic in the first half of the set, while in the second half he would demonstrate spirit rapping – taps on a table which some believed to be messages from the dead – and other spiritualist techniques to show that they could be performed without supernatural aid.

A key element of John's mystique was his ability to perform tricks outside of his performances, away from the theatre, often in a spontaneous attempt to promote his tours. One time he came across a boy crying by the River Thames. He and his mother had fallen on hard times so she had sent him to her former employer to beg for some money. The man had given the boy a sovereign[3] to give to his mother. On his way home, the boy had been distracted by anglers on the river. Leaning out to get a closer look, the sovereign fell from his grasp into the water. On hearing this story, John borrowed a fishing rod from one of the anglers and caught a perch. He told the boy to look under the gills of the fish – where he found a shiny gold sovereign. John presented the boy with another sovereign and sent him on his way, much to the amazement of all watching.

Ironically, John himself was almost bankrupt at this point. He often struggled with money, due to financial speculations and misfortune, such as when the American Civil War curtailed his tour of the United States. The theatre he built in Glasgow burned down after only a few months. This lack of money may have contributed to his relatively early death, aged 60, at a time when he was worried by financial troubles.

Perhaps John's best-known trick was the Great Gun Trick or the Bullet Catch. Although he was not the one to

---

[3] Equivalent to approximately £120 nowadays.

create the trick, he certainly helped to popularise it. This trick involved an audience member firing a loaded gun at him. Instead of being struck down by the bullet, he would catch it, miraculously unharmed. The way that he performed this trick was through sleight of hand: after he had shown the bullet to some members of the audience, he would switch it for one that felt like the real thing but would blow apart when the gun was fired.

Not that the trick was without risk – as he discovered in 1844 when he was performing at London's Adelphi Theatre. The man chosen as the shooter stepped forward and took the bullet off John before he could perform the switch. He loaded the gun and stood ready to fire, with a smug expression which made John realise that he had worked out how the trick was done. The shooter wanted to expose him in front of an audience but, always one for theatricality, John decided to face him down. Without any sign of agitation, he tapped his chest and said to the man: 'Aim here – and fire when you wish.'

John gave a half-smile as he waited, seemingly calmly, for the man to make his move. Tension radiated through the room. The marksman raised the gun. He tightened the trigger. Yet he waited to fire. It was a game of chicken – and if neither of them gave in, John would die.

Instead, the shooter's nerve broke. He allowed the gun muzzle to fall. Before the man could change his mind, John swooped down upon him, gently ushering him back to his seat in the audience and asking for a new volunteer. John unloaded the gun, ostensibly to allow the new shooter to load it himself but, in reality, to make the switch. The trick went off without a hitch and he 'caught' the bullet. Although the audience was not consciously aware that John had been in actual danger of his life, they broke into riotous applause, fuelled by the more-than-usual tension in the air.

This story sums up John: his daring, his showmanship and his ability to turn disaster into triumph. One can certainly see why a young Houdini, also an adroit self-promoter, was such an admirer of his Scottish predecessor's work that he decided to pay his burial site a visit.

2. ELIZABETH AND ALEXANDER BLACKWELL

Botanical Illustrator and her Chancer Husband/Brother

c. 1700 - 1758 and c. 1700 - 1748

On the surface, the story of Elizabeth and Alexander Blackwell is one replicated often through the course of history: a loyal but long-suffering wife is forced to endure the consequences of her capricious husband's actions. However, theirs is given novelty by the unusual details: incest, a stay in a debtors' prison, the first female botanical illustrator and execution for treason.

Alexander and Elizabeth were among the many children of the Reverend Thomas Blackwell, the Principal at Marischal College. As a young woman, Elizabeth became pregnant, probably by her elder brother Thomas. A baby born out of wedlock was a huge scandal; one born of incest would have destroyed Reverend Thomas's career and social position. The family hushed up the affair and the baby was passed off as another of the Reverend's children. Elizabeth's prospects would not have been good. Her family would probably have blamed her for what had happened and she would have been kept under close supervision, never able to escape from her elder brother and possible-abuser Thomas.

Elizabeth decided to flee to London with her brother Alexander, who gave up his studies as a medical student. Once in London, they lived as husband and wife, to all appearances a devoted couple who had been forced to elope by a hard-hearted family. Their secret was safe for centuries until Alexander Cruden[4] biographer Julia Keay did some historical detective work and discovered that Elizabeth was not, as had long been supposed, Alexander's cousin but his sister.

Alexander's first enterprise in London was a printing business. His initial success soon encountered the ire of rival publishers who resented that Alexander had not served the mandatory four-year printer's apprenticeship. He defended himself against the subsequent legal action but this left him heavily in debt and he was thrown in Highgate Prison by a creditor.

Elizabeth was forced to draw on her own resources to support herself and their child, as well as to pay off Alexander's debts and have him released from prison. She was aware that there was a gap in the medical textbook market: namely a modern 'herbal', a book which would illustrate all of the relevant medicinal herbs and plants along with their uses. Many new species had recently been discovered, particularly in the Americas and a reference book which included these plants would be highly sought-after. She submitted drawings to several leading doctors and apothecaries; they were so impressed that they encouraged her to hire a house near Chelsea Physic Garden so that she could always see fresh specimens.

Once a drawing was completed, she would take it to her brother in prison. There he would give her information on the foreign names of the plant, as well as its medicinal properties. From 1737 to 1739 she released four plates a week until she had produced 500 drawings and descriptions. This was a phenomenal undertaking. Normally a piece of work on this scale would require at least three skilled craftsmen: one to make the initial drawing, another to engrave the copper plates used to print the pages and the third to delicately hand-colour each image. Elizabeth did all of this by herself, as well as being intimately involved in

---

[4] See 7. Alexander Cruden.

both printing and promotion, striking deals with booksellers to heighten her chances of success.

The completed work was published in two volumes and sold well from the start. Elizabeth had been right to think that such a book was desperately needed by those working on the frontline of medicine. It was not only a success in Britain but was known across Europe and was used by doctors and apothecaries well into the 19th century. It was considered of greater use than more scientific texts because of the accuracy of the drawings and the number of illustrations of new plants.

What all this success meant in real terms for Elizabeth was that she could pay Alexander's debts and have him released from prison. Initially, he appears to have settled back into normal life, taking pride in the status afforded to him as the husband of this acclaimed author. He became interested in agricultural improvements and even wrote his own treatise on improving wet and clayey soil. On the back of this, he was asked to advise the Duke of Chandos on some work on his estate. However, it was not long before Alexander slipped back into bad habits, making some unwise business decisions. Struggling to escape a new collection of debts, he once again needed his sister to bail him out - this time, Elizabeth had to sell off part of the herbal's publication rights to settle his obligations.

But Alexander had a stroke of luck. His fame as an agricultural consultant had spread to Scandinavia and the Swedish court offered him a job. In 1742 he set sail for Stockholm and when he arrived was invited to stay at the Prime Minister's house and given a pension. An even greater stroke of luck befell him when the King of Sweden, Frederick I, became very ill and Alexander was allowed to prescribe for him. His treatment miraculously worked, the King made a full recovery and Alexander was appointed one of the royal physicians. He took to calling himself a doctor, despite not having completed a degree in medicine. The Swedish court soon found out that his medical knowledge was greatly lacking and instead he was given charge of a model farm. It would appear this farm was unsuccessful under his supervision.

Elizabeth never saw him again. While he was away, she kept sending him a portion of the profits from the herbal and it is said that she and her child were due to sail to Sweden when Alexander's luck ran out. In March 1747 he presented himself to King Frederick saying that he had received a message from the Queen of Denmark (who was also King George II of Britain's daughter) saying that if Frederick excluded his heir from the succession, a large sum of money would be forthcoming. Although the King initially seemed interested, the next day he had grown worried by this intrigue and Alexander was arrested. When questioned, Alexander said that he had received an anonymous letter containing this information but added that he had subsequently destroyed the evidence.

It was a dangerous time to get involved in Swedish politics. There were two factions at court, with one sect eager to align themselves with France while the other wanted a closer alliance with Britain. Alexander appeared to be intriguing on behalf of Britain. He was accused of plotting to overthrow the constitution and alter the line of succession: in other words, treason. Under torture, he confessed to this crime.

He was sentenced to be broken on the wheel, a particularly nasty punishment and considered a great dishonour.[5] When he was sentenced it was implied that the plot had been to remove the Crown Prince from the line of succession, poison the next heir and place the Duke of Cumberland (King George II's younger son) on the throne.

The bizarre thing about this is that no one else was implicated in this plot. The British government withdrew

---

[5] Breaking on the wheel is best known for being the intended punishment of St Catherine of Alexandria, giving us the term 'Catherine wheel' for the firework.

their ambassador from Stockholm in outrage at the accusations levelled at their monarch and did everything they could to throw the blame on Alexander and distance themselves from him – perhaps a sign that they were involved. Historians have speculated that Swedish prime minister Count Tessin may have been behind the letter, attempting to get rid of a man who held the King's favour by having him found guilty of treason. But perhaps the most likely explanation is that Alexander concocted the whole thing himself: seeing his standing at the Swedish court decline, as they became aware of his shortcomings as both a doctor and a farmer, he sought to make himself relevant again by winning the King over to this scheme. It would seem like a bizarre explanation for most people's behaviour in such circumstances – but it seems to fit with Alexander, something of a chancer whose schemes rarely worked out in the long run.

Alexander was executed in 1748, not by the wheel but through a far more merciful beheading. Little is known of the rest of Elizabeth's life, other than that she died in Chelsea 10 years later. Historians speculate that she lived the rest of her life quietly, near to the gardens which had made her name. Even so, by the time of her death, she would have been aware that her book was a huge success and had greatly contributed to medical and botanical knowledge at the time. Despite a life dominated by incestuous relationships with her own exploitative brothers, she is remembered for her own achievements in a traditionally male field.

Alexander does not come across well in this biography. But a story from the end of his life gives an insight into his witty and quick-thinking personality. As Alexander was about to be executed, he put his head on the block the wrong way and had to be corrected. Apologising, he joked that as it was his first time being executed, it was no wonder that he required a little instruction. He may have been a chancer, but he was certainly an entertaining one.

3. THOMAS BLAKE GLOVER

Industrial Revolutionary in Japan

1838 - 1911

Despite being rebranded as the 'Scottish Samurai' in the late 20th century, Thomas Blake Glover was neither a samurai nor particularly Scottish. A hard-drinking, drug-trafficking, prostitute-using colonial opportunist is best remembered in his native Aberdeenshire for helping to industrialise Japan. Less is said about his own vices or how his work laid the foundations of Japan as a military power, leading to its role in the Second World War.

Thomas was typical of so many young men who travelled to the furthest reaches of the British Empire to take advantage of colonial inequalities and make his fortune. Born in Fraserburgh, the son of a coastguard officer, he received a solid education at the Gymnasium School in Old Aberdeen. At the age of 19, he got a job with Jardine Matheson, which was one of the largest British trading companies working out of the Far East at the time. A sign of their influence can be seen in the fact that they successfully lobbied the British government to fight the First Opium War in 1840.

When Thomas arrived in Shanghai in 1857, the Second Opium War was ongoing. Thanks to these wars, British traders were dominant in the city, mainly trading in tea, silk and opium. Given that the drug was illegal in China, British ships transporting it from India would offload their cargo on to other vessels before passing through customs. One of Thomas' jobs was to check the supplies of opium and prepare it for distribution.

Shanghai was a brilliant place for an ambitious young man to make a fortune, often by operating outside the bounds of the law. However, Japan – just opening up to Western trade – held even more potential. In 1853, US ships had arrived in Japan, ending 200 years of 'sakoku' or 'locked country'. Under sakoku, no foreigners (except for some Chinese emissaries) could enter the country or else they would be beheaded. If a Japanese person was caught trying to leave the country, they would be condemned to death without trial, often through ritual suicide.

In 1859, the Ansei (or 'unequal') Treaties were signed which greatly benefited imperial foreign powers, for example by opening up several Japanese port cities to international trade. They also allowed Japan's trading partners, not Japan, to determine what the import-export taxes should be. Two-and-a-half months after the treaties came into effect, Thomas arrived in Nagasaki on behalf of Jardine Matheson. It was still an incredibly dangerous time to be a foreigner in Japan. Many of the samurai clans remained deeply committed to keeping Japan 'pure' through 'joi' or 'ethnic cleansing'. Attacks were made on several merchants and in 1863, the US Consulate was burned down.

However, it was also a very profitable time to be a foreign trader. Japan had shut itself off to outside influence for such a long time that its technology had not advanced in the same way as the West and it had hardly industrialised at all. In addition, there were significant tensions between the Shogun (the effective rulers of the country) and the clans who wanted the Emperor to return to power. The latter groups were more open to embracing new technologies and weapons, exchanging their samurai swords for guns. It was these same clans who were committed to the idea of joi, making them very dangerous business partners. However, Thomas could see that they were more invested in restoring the Emperor to power than ridding the country of foreigners. He took the bold move of reaching out to these clans, first building relationships with the Satsuma clan and then the more joi-committed Choshu clan, who had been behind the attack on the US Consulate.

Thomas did not entirely throw in his lot with the clans. He was a cautious businessman and both the Japanese and British governments designated these groups as terrorists. Instead, being the savvy entrepreneur that he was, Thomas, who had set up his own company after two years, kept on selling weapons to both sides.

It is often said that he smuggled the Choshu Five – a group of young noblemen who wanted to receive a Western education, including future Prime Minister Ito Hirobumi and future Foreign Minister Inoue Kaoru – out of Japan. This would have been far too political an action for Thomas at this stage, but he did help organise their visit to Britain, encouraging Jardine Matheson to pay their expenses and getting his brother to meet Ito and Inoue at Southampton. He became good friends with the former, who even taught him a few samurai moves in the garden of Thomas' house in Nagasaki, though this was probably as close as Thomas ever got to becoming a samurai.

The Choshu Five were the first Japanese students to make this journey and several others soon followed suit. Thomas played a far more active role in helping the Satsuma Nineteen travel to Britain in 1865. The Nineteen all spent time studying in the UK, some staying for only a year and some for up to ten years. The youngest member of the group was Nagasawa Kanae, a boy in his early teens. Too young to go to university, he stayed with the Glover family at Braehead House in Aberdeen and studied at Thomas' old school, the Gym, coming first in his year in English grammar and reading. Thanks to Thomas, several other Japanese students made the trip to Aberdeen: in 1866, a third of Japanese students in the UK were in Aberdeen.

Back in the Far East, the clans ended up banding together, overthrowing the Shogun and restoring the Emperor. In the wake of the civil war, which ended in 1869, Thomas continued living in Japan but his work in the country started to change: instead of being focused purely on opportunities to sell, he began developing ideas that invested in the country. He developed Japan's first Western-style coal mine. He also played a role in the formation of Mitsubishi: he was friends with the first and second presidents and worked as an advisor to the company for almost 35 years. In some cases, by helping Japan to develop industrially, he harmed his own business enterprises. He built the country's first dry dock, meaning that modern ships could be built in Japan, rather than made in Britain and sold through a broker like Thomas.

Perhaps his most celebrated business venture is the establishment of the Japanese Brewing Company, famous for making Kirin, which is the oldest beer brand in Japan. Thomas' daughter Hana drew the artwork for the original bottle, which depicted a mythical creature called a 'kirin'. In 1907 when Mitsubishi bought the company, they added a long droopy moustache to the creature as a reference to Thomas' facial hair. When Thomas set up the company, he volunteered to pay taxes, even though as a foreigner he had no legal obligation to do so. The Japanese Brewing Company was the only foreign-owned company to pay tax during this time.

Thomas also became a critic of the Ansei Treaties, which were established to benefit British trade. Unfortunately for him, he had made his home in Japan and, while there were many benefits from the Treaties, they also prevented him from travelling anywhere in the country apart from a couple of other port cities. In addition, his wife was denied any rights while she lived with him in the British settlement in Nagasaki.

Thomas' wife Tsuru was an upper-class prostitute who had permission to visit the British settlement. Their 'marriage' was a ceremony which gave legal recognition to her right to live with Thomas in the British compound. Although Thomas was certainly not faithful to her, he appears to have loved her and considered the marriage binding: he always referred to her as his wife or 'Mrs Glover', they spent around 30 years together and when they found she could have no more children, they adopted Thomas' son, Tomisaburo, whom he had with another woman.

Sometimes Thomas is said to be the inspiration behind the opera *Madama Butterfly*, where a US naval officer enters into a marriage of convenience with a young Japanese woman whom he abandons shortly after. But this is not particularly reflective of Thomas and Tsuru's relationship, especially given his devastation after her death. It is thought that the mistake was made because Thomas' Nagasaki mansion may have been given the nickname 'Madame Butterfly House' by American troops occupying the city after the Second World War.

Sadly for Thomas, it was only after Tsuru's death that he was allowed to move freely around Japan. In the last few years of his life, when his health had greatly declined, he was awarded the Order of the Rising Sun, second class. He was the first foreign national to be so highly decorated, a sign of how significant he has been to Japanese industrialisation.

He died in Japan aged 73, something he surely never would have anticipated when he arrived there, looking to get rich quick, some 50 years previously. Despite maintaining his British identity throughout his life, he chose to be buried in Japan, the country he had made his home.

4. WALFORD BODIE

'Electric Wizard' and Quack Doctor

1869 - 1939

A woman's hair stands on end. A couple kiss and sparks literally fly. Electricity flows through a man's body. As it does, cigarettes, gas jets and lightbulbs are all lit just by being held near him. All of this was a common sight at one of 'Dr' Walford Bodie's shows.

Walford was born Samuel Murphy Bodie, the son of a baker in Aberdeen. He left school at 14 to work for the Scottish National Telephone Company, which provided him with training in how electricity worked – something that he would go on to use to great effect. From a young age, he had been performing sleight of hand and ventriloquism, giving his first proper performance at Stonehaven Town Hall. At the age of 17, he met Jeannie Henry at a show in Banff. She became his wife, and she and her sisters became Walford's assistants, with Isabella Henry taking what was probably the most important role: La Belle Electra.

Walford's shows involved a lot of hypnosis, both of his assistants and audience members. Volunteers would flap like chickens or grunt like pigs. In the intervals, men would be hypnotised into hopping around the theatre. The story goes that at a performance in North Wales, one hopping man left the theatre and was arrested by a policeman because he would not stop bouncing. To drum up publicity for a show in Aberdeen, Walford hypnotised a person who then lay sleeping in a coffin in a shop window for an entire week. At Dundee Zoo, he entered a cage of savage hyenas and managed to subdue them with hypnosis. On another occasion, La Belle Electra was hypnotised, placed in a coffin and buried six feet underground. She was left there for 20 minutes before being dug out. She appeared completely unshaken by this experience.

But above all, Walford was known for his use of electricity. In 1890, William Kemmler was executed at New York's Sing Sing prison, thus becoming the first person in the world to die by electric chair. Walford decided to have his own replica chair built which he incorporated into the show. In 1920, he was delighted when his friend Harry Houdini presented him with the original Sing Sing electric chair which soon became his new prop.[6]

The 'Electric Wizard' capitalised on the fact that electricity was still a very mysterious thing to the general population. He would sit on his electric chair and experience a high level of voltage but a low current. He claimed that he could withstand 240 million volts, which was highly impressive to his audiences who did not realise that – despite the sparks that were flying all around – this was relatively safe.

To add to the impression that this was something that only he or La Belle Electra could withstand, he would offer audience members a chance to have a go in the chair. They were promised that they would get 10 shillings (the equivalent to 50p nowadays) for every 30 seconds they were able to sit in the chair.

When any audience members attempted to do so, Walford would increase the current. Their lips might turn blue, their bodies would shake and some of them would even lose consciousness – soon restored to rights after several slaps administered by the 'doctor'. It was a brilliant demonstration of Walford's point that death by electricity was unnecessarily cruel.

---

[6] To read about Houdini's connection to another Aberdeen magician, see 1. John Henry Anderson.

However, in 1906, one audience member managed to get the better of Walford. James Wright, an electrician from Blackburn, rigged up a special suit with copper and asbestos, meaning that he could sit quite comfortably in the chair without being affected by the currents. James later claimed that Walford was so angry at being thwarted that his assistants had dragged James offstage and removed his clothes to reveal how he was able to withstand the chair.

As well as demonstrating the dangers of electricity, Walford was quick to advocate it as a healing device. He claimed that through his combination of electricity, hypnosis and massage, he could cure previously paralysed limbs. In one of his books, Walford reproduces a before-and-after picture of a man with a wasted arm who, he claimed, was unable to lift a feather before Walford's treatment. The after photograph shows the man holding a 56 lb (25 kg) weight, although we only have Walford's word that he was not able to do so before. Outside the theatres where he performed were piles of walking sticks and crutches, supposedly discarded by all the people whom he had cured. He claimed that over the course of his career he cured more than 900 people, though perhaps there was a placebo effect at work. Some Walford fans point out that he never charged anyone to treat them and would mainly focus his attention on the poor.

Having said that, he did profit from some of his medical cures. He allowed his name to be used in advertising for products such as 'electric pills' and 'electric ointment', in return for a share in the profits. He also controversially used the title 'doctor', as well as a whole string of letters after his name, including MD, meaning Medicinae Doctor or Doctor of Medicine. The medical establishment was infuriated by this quackery and in 1909 bankrolled Charles Henry Irving, a disgruntled former assistant of Walford's, to bring a court case against him.

Although the case was officially about the fact that Charles had paid Walford £1,000 to learn his profession,

Walford's qualifications came up in court. Despite having previously claimed that he received his medical degree in the United States, he admitted in court that he had bought his certificates from a Bradford dentist and claimed 'showman's privilege' as an excuse for his deception. When asked about the use of the letters 'MD', he argued that they stood for 'Merrie Devil', a nickname given him by the London theatre proprietors.

The case went against Walford and he was ordered to pay Charles £1,000. Ever the self-promoter, he produced a new poster about his 'great victory', highlighting the fact that 30,000 volts had passed through his body in front of a jury. He continued to use the title 'doctor', even in that very poster.

Shortly afterwards, Walford was performing at the Coliseum in Glasgow when medical students started throwing rotten vegetables and eggs at him. The orchestra fled and after some failed attempts to reconcile with the students, the police cleared the theatre. Several participants in these 'Bodie Riots' were brought to court and fined, although it was suspected that these fines might have been paid by their professors, who perhaps were the ones really behind the riot.

In the wake of this, Walford had a nervous breakdown and cancelled several shows. Some say that from then on he always avoided playing to big crowds and big theatres but perhaps the truth is just that these events coincided with his decline in popularity.

The pre-First World War period may be considered the peak of Walford's career. Theatregoers were easily impressed by the sparks of electricity. His fame was such that he and his pointy moustache were parodied by a young Charlie Chaplin in his music hall performances. By 1905, Walford had made enough money to build his own mansion, the Manor House in Macduff.

During the First World War, he struggled with depleted audiences. He went on tour to South Africa, India and

Ceylon (now Sri Lanka). On the way back, the ship he was travelling on was torpedoed and, although everyone on board was rescued, the equipment for his show ended up at the bottom of the ocean. Walford suffered a second stroke of bad luck when his next ship was also torpedoed, this time in the Mediterranean, though eventually Walford and his family made it back to Britain.

This was not the end of his misfortune. La Belle Electra died in 1919 after an accident with the electric chair which caused her to receive too large a jolt of electricity. His wife Jeannie never really recovered from the torpedoing of the ship. She died in 1931, having seen their daughter and one of their sons die before her.

Still, 'The Most Remarkable Man on Earth', as he billed himself, was not one to be knocked back for long. The last decade of his life saw a revival in his fortunes. Eighteen months after Jeannie's death, he married a dancer 40 years his junior named Florrie Robertshaw. By the 1930s, he owned six guest houses, two hotels, a flat and a house in London, as well as the manor in Macduff. In fact, he owned so much property that his pet monkey was able to have its own suite of rooms. His favourite place, though, was probably his houseboat on the Thames where he hosted lavish parties, regularly attended by Edward, the Prince of Wales and his lover Wallis Simpson. Appropriately the boat was called La Belle Electra, named after Walford's most famous assistant, but also a reference to the electricity that had made his name.

5. JAMES BURNETT, LORD MONBODDO

Eccentric Enlightenment Thinker

1714 - 1799

James Burnett was a judge in Scotland's highest civil court, a learned lawyer who had studied with the leading legal scholars of his day and was a researcher into historical linguistics with an interest in early ideas about evolution. He is, however, best remembered for believing that orangutans were part of the human species. He claimed that humans used to have tails because 130 years before a Swedish captain said that he had discovered a society of tailed humans in the Bay of Bengal. In his day, James was mocked by his contemporaries who said he lurked outside rooms where births were taking place in the hope of seeing a baby before its tail was removed by the midwife.

Coincidentally James made his name as a lawyer through a case that hinged on what had taken place in a birthing room.

The Douglas Cause split the country. The case was in front of the Scottish courts for five years and took seven years in total to be resolved. The question to be settled was who should inherit the Duke of Douglas's estates, one of the most valuable in Scotland. His nearest male heir was his nephew Archibald, a boy of 14 years old. However, the Duke of Hamilton, Douglas's cousin, claimed that Archibald was not actually a Douglas.

Some suspicious circumstances surrounded his birth. The Duke of Douglas's sister, Jane, had secretly married Colonel John Stewart, a penniless adventurer. She had concealed this marriage from her brother, fearing that he would disapprove and cut off her allowance. The newlyweds set off for Europe and two years later, in Paris, 50-year-old Jane gave birth to twin boys: Sholto and Archibald. Sholto died as an infant but Archibald survived. Jane eventually told her brother about the marriage but he refused to believe that the children were hers.

This meant the estates probably would have gone to the Hamiltons, had it not been for a last-minute reversal. In the final years of his life, the Duke of Douglas surprised everyone by at last marrying. His bride was a distant relation called Margaret Douglas. She tirelessly pleaded with him to acknowledge his nephew and, 10 days before he died, he did.

The Hamiltons were furious at missing out on the inheritance and despatched an investigator to France. He came back with the information that the babies were not Jane's real children and had been kidnapped: one the son of a glassmaker; the other the child of a rope dancer. At that point, the lawyers got involved.

The case grabbed public attention and everyone had an opinion: leading Enlightenment figures Adam Smith and David Hume supported the Hamiltons; Samuel Johnson biographer James Boswell broke away from his mentor and sided with the Douglases.

For five years, the lawyers slugged it out in the Scottish courts, with both sides spending more than £54,000.[7] James was one of the lawyers appearing for the Douglas family. He went to Paris three times to collect evidence and it is probably because of his persistence that the family eventually won their case in the House of Lords in 1769.

James perhaps summed up best why people unconnected with the families felt so passionately about the case. He argued that everything in the Douglas case suggested Archibald was the biological nephew of the Duke of Douglas: his parents said he was their son, as did the staff

---

[7] The equivalent of almost £9 million nowadays.

of their household; Jane's affection for her children was described as maternal; and Archibald and Sholto were said to resemble their parents. With all this evidence to support something normally accepted without doubt – namely, that a mother can be believed about her children – James argued that not to believe it would set a precedent of no one being sure about anything.

When the case was finally settled, it caused a reaction across the country. In Edinburgh, a mob gathered, demanding that all the houses be lit up in honour of Archibald Douglas's victory and smashing the windows of those Law Lords who had voted against him. This went on for two nights and soldiers eventually had to settle the riot.

The case also helped launch James's career: after four years working for the Douglases, he was elevated to the bench of the Court of Session and became Lord Monboddo, named for his family estates in Aberdeenshire.

Despite his profession being the law, it was not his passion. He was particularly interested in language and believed that it had evolved, arguing that humans were nothing more than wild animals until the ability to communicate had been developed. He believed Greek and Sanskrit had been invented by philosophers and were the only languages free from 'barbarity'. Some see the seeds of Darwinism in his belief that humans should be studied like wild animals.

But as part of his belief in evolution, he also believed that humans had degenerated. He tried to live simply, as the Ancient Greeks would have done, taking cold baths and exercising naked. When on the Monboddo estate near Laurencekirk, he dressed as a farmer and was noted for never increasing his tenants' rent. Because the Greeks had not used carriages or sedan chairs, he also refused to do so, and instead insisted on riding on horseback, no matter how horrible the weather.

It was believed that this rejection of carriages might have led to his second daughter Elizabeth's early death from tuberculosis. After her death, the poet Robert Burns wrote *Elegy on the late Miss Burnet of Monboddo*, praising her youth, beauty and mind. She had appeared in previous poems of his and after Burns had first met her, he was asked by an acquaintance whether he admired her. He responded: 'I admired God Almighty more than ever. Miss Burnett is the most heavenly of all his works.'

Although it may have killed his daughter, cold baths and riding in the rain appeared to have little impact on James's health: he lived until he was 85. Even into his 80s, he would ride to London to spend a couple of weeks there every year. Only on one occasion did he agree to ride in a friend's carriage and that was after he had fallen ill on his very last trip to the capital. But the very next day, he was atop his horse once again to continue the journey.

It was on a trip to London that he displayed his eccentric credentials to their utmost when visiting the Court of the King's Bench. By this point, his eyesight and hearing were failing and he did not notice as the ceiling began to collapse. Everybody rushed out of the building, but James remained seated. After being safely evacuated, he was asked why he had not fled the building with everyone else. He replied that he had assumed it was 'an annual ceremony, with which, as an alien, he had nothing to do'.

6. GEORGE GORDON BYRON, 6TH BARON BYRON

Mad, Bad and Dangerous to Know

1788 - 1824

'Half a Scot by birth, and bred a whole one,' is how Lord Byron described himself in his poem *Don Juan*. Although many people think of Byron as an English Romantic poet, he was a self-defined Scot and spent his formative years in Aberdeen.

His mother was Catherine Gordon, a direct descendant of King James I of Scotland. She was a wealthy heiress and grew up in Banff under the supervision of her grandmother. With £23,000[8] to her name, a headstrong manner and no parents, she was the perfect target for fortune hunters. In 1785, she took herself off to Bath to find a husband.

It was there that she met Captain John Byron, known as 'Mad Jack' to his army buddies because of his outrageous gambling. Mad Jack already had one marriage behind him. He had seduced Amelia Osbourne, Marchioness of Carmarthen, convincing her to run away with him and divorce her husband, a highly unusual course of action in the 18th century. Amelia died after five years, leaving one daughter, Augusta.

Mad Jack was now in desperate need of funds, with creditors snapping at his heels, no more friends to borrow from and a father who had disinherited him. Four months after meeting, Catherine and Jack married. He soon ran through her fortune and sold her estate, Gight Castle. They separated not long after and Catherine gave birth to George

---

[8] The equivalent of £3.5 million nowadays.

Gordon Byron in January 1788. Catherine returned to Scotland with her new-born son and they settled in Aberdeen in 1790. Mad Jack turned up in Aberdeen briefly, looking for more money, and when Catherine had borrowed enough to give him, he left for France, never to see his son again as he died 11 months later.

Catherine raised her son in a flat on Broad Street in Aberdeen. She was said to have a fiery temper which she passed on to her son. The young George once got so angry that he bit into a china plate – a plate that was for many years treasured by one Aberdonian family as a souvenir of George's time in the city.

George was studying at Aberdeen Grammar School when his great-uncle, the 5th Baron Byron, died. Since his father was dead, George inherited the title, and he and his mother left Aberdeen for Newstead Abbey, which was now his.

After moving to Nottinghamshire, George only once returned to the North East. When he was around 15 years old, he played truant for several weeks and came back to Aberdeenshire to climb Lochnagar, near Balmoral. This mountain is the subject of one of Byron's poems, while other Aberdonian landmarks such as the Rivers Dee and Don and the Brig o' Balgownie also make appearances.

Nowadays, George is not particularly well-known for his poetry. He is far better remembered for being a larger-than-life character and the tagline so often used to describe him: 'mad, bad and dangerous to know'. This description was first applied to George by Lady Caroline Lamb. She and George had an affair that lasted one summer. Afterwards, Lady Caroline seems to have been unable to get over him, despite being a married woman. She burnt his effigy on a bonfire and attempted to stab him at a party. She sent him a parcel containing her pubic hair, along with a note saying that it was from 'your wild gazelle', apologising for the blood as she had 'cut the hair too close' and asking for him to send some blood back in return.

She was not the only woman who became obsessed with the fashionable poet and his 'Byronic' good looks. Nor was she the only one to send him hair. His fans would regularly send him locks of their hair and ask him to respond in kind. George instead would send them hair clipped from his dog.

George seems to have loved animals far more than any person. When he attended Trinity College, Cambridge, he was not allowed to take his dog Smut with him as dogs were not allowed in university rooms. George dealt with that problem by bringing a tame bear instead. When another pet dog called Boatswain got rabies, George nursed him without worrying that he might be bitten and die of the disease himself. After Boatswain died, George erected a massive monument to him on his estate.

Such actions have gone down in history as part of the Byron legend. Another bizarre incident was when his gardener found a skull buried on his estate, probably one of the monks who had lived there when it was still an abbey. George had the skull made into a drinking vessel and he would fill it with claret and pass it around his guests at parties.

George left Britain in 1816 and never returned. One reason for his self-imposed exile was the rumours about his close relationship with his half-sister, Augusta. It was whispered that Augusta's daughter Medora was also George's child and that the pair had been having an incestuous affair. Whether that was the case or not, George's sexual exploits would shock even nowadays. He had numerous affairs with youths and boys, some as young as 14.

Even his marriage was unconventional: he married Annabella Milbanke in 1815 and they were together for one year and 13 days when she, fearing that George was insane and shocked by his descriptions of his debauchery, returned to her parents with their new-born baby. They never saw each other again. Annabella prevented her daughter from studying poetry or literature, in the hope that she would not follow in her father's footsteps. Instead, thanks to an education that eschewed the arts and pursued the sciences so rigorously, Ada Lovelace became a gifted mathematician and is now widely regarded as the world's first computer programmer.

Despite all of this, George did have some good qualities. His political views were liberal and forward-thinking. While in the House of Lords, he spoke out against the death penalty for Luddites and in favour of Catholics receiving the vote.

In later years, he became a passionate advocate for Greek independence from the Ottoman empire, moving to Greece to fight for the cause and supplying a considerable amount of money. But his support for independence did not prevent him from seeing the humanity of the other side. One of his last actions before he died, probably of sepsis, was to release some Turkish prisoners, including a young girl called Hato, who would otherwise have been killed by Greek nationalists. But such acts of compassion do not sell books and it is far more entertaining to remember the numerous occasions when George lived up to his mad, bad and dangerous-to-know persona.

7. ALEXANDER CRUDEN

A 'Madman' who Created a Go-to Scholarly Aid

1699 - 1770

Beaten, purged and forcibly subjected to bloodletting. Restrained by handcuffs, chained to his bed, and made to wear a 'strait-waistcoat' so that he was forced to eat his meals 'with his mouth like a dog'. Not allowed to change his clothes or wash for five straight weeks. These were just some of the forms of torture Alexander Cruden had to endure during a two-and-a-half-month stay in a private madhouse in London in 1738.

The situation was probably made far worse by this being the second time he was incarcerated against his will on the grounds of insanity. In total, he was imprisoned for madness four times. Yet Alexander posed no danger to himself or those around him. Although his behaviour was eccentric and he often flouted convention, he was also a deeply pious and compassionate man who just a year before had completed one of the most significant aids to biblical study ever created in the English language.

After Alexander had been incarcerated for 23 days, he was told that he would be released if he signed a letter absolving the man who had put him there of any wrongdoing. Alexander steadfastly refused to do so. Finally, after almost 10 miserable weeks in the madhouse, he managed to obtain his freedom. Using the knife with which he ate his dinner, he cut through the bedstead which he was chained to. It took him four days to whittle his way through the wood and his hands broke out in painful blisters.

Once he had removed the chain from the bed, Alexander jumped out of the garden window and climbed over the back wall, all the while carrying the chain that was still attached to his leg. Barefoot and bleeding, he wandered through an unfamiliar area of London until he was detained by some constables for being a suspicious character. Despite his unusual appearance, he managed to convince them not to send him back to the madhouse and he was allowed to present his case to the Lord Mayor, who ruled that he should be released.

Historians have argued about whether or not Alexander really was 'mad'. In the 18th century, anyone could be 'put away' to a private madhouse, as long as the person committing them had the money to pay for their upkeep. In this case, Alexander had been committed by his romantic rival Robert Wrightman, a fellow suitor for the hand of a wealthy widow.

This man had somehow learned about the first time Alexander had been incarcerated for madness, when he was a young man studying at Marischal College to become a clergyman. At the same time, he was courting Elizabeth Blackwell,[9] the daughter of Marischal's principal, Reverend Thomas Blackwell. But it later turned out that Elizabeth was pregnant by her own brother. Some historians think that Alexander found this out and that was why he was put into the Aberdeen Tolbooth for madness. It was an attempt by Elizabeth's influential father to discredit anything Alexander might say about his daughter. If that was indeed the case, it worked. Because of this, Alexander had to give up his hopes of a career as a minister and leave Aberdeen. He eventually settled in London where he became a proof-reader.

Whether or not Alexander was mad, he was certainly an unusual man. The last time he was committed to an asylum was by his sister Isabella. She did so after Alexander had attempted to break up a brawl. He then spent the next hour telling the men off for swearing and occasionally hitting them over the head with a shovel.

---

[9] See 2. Elizabeth and Alexander Blackwell.

It seems that after he was released from a madhouse for the last time, he embraced his eccentricities and the fact that he would never be seen as entirely normal. He gave himself a new name: Alexander the Corrector. He had been working as a proof-reader or 'corrector'; now he would be a corrector of people. He would go around correcting bad behaviour, telling people off for swearing or not observing the Sabbath. He carried with him a sponge to remove political graffiti that he disagreed with.

As he wanted 'Alexander the Corrector' to be made official, he went to court in the hope that the king would make it his title. He wrote that he was largely ignored but that the Earl of Paulet was polite to him 'for, being goutish in his feet, he could not run away'.

Alexander had a very different way of looking at the world. Rather than madness, it perhaps could be best characterised as blind or even groundless optimism, coupled with an ignorance of social mores. This extended to his relationships with women. He would propose to women whom he had no romantic connection with and, in one case, had never even met. He refused to take no for an answer. When the daughter of the mayor of London turned him down, he wrote her a 'declaration of war' and sent 'prayer bullets' as part of his campaign: prayers that he sent to all the churches she might visit while on holiday in the hope that they would be read out from the pulpit and she would hear his name.

But his inability to quite figure out how the world worked was in some cases a boon. On one occasion, he became aware of the case of a sailor who was sentenced to be executed for forgery. Alexander was convinced that the man had been taken advantage of by another sailor and had not intended to commit a crime. Although the sentence was due to be carried out in two days' time, Alexander relentlessly petitioned the Secretary of State and managed to get the sentence reduced to deportation. It was extremely rare for a sentence to be reduced this close to the scheduled execution. Anyone but Alexander would probably have given up hope.

Another instance of Alexander's unusual world view proving to be a force for good was when he was solicited by a prostitute on the street. He took pity on the poor woman. Anyone else might just have given her money and walked away. Not Alexander. He offered her a job as his housekeeper. Apparently, this was a success; we are told that she worked for him until he died.

Alexander may have had an unconventional world view, but that gave him the ability to achieve things no one else did. In his day he was considered a madman. But more importantly, he was also an incredibly kind man. His lasting impression of the madhouse where he was incarcerated for 10 weeks was not the cruelty of his tormentors, but his own failings in wanting to get as far away as possible from the other inmates, rather than seeking ways to alleviate their sufferings. To atone for this moral failing, he became a passionate advocate of prison reform and brought food, clothing and medicine to prisoners in Newgate, a prison that had been compared to a sewer. It is to be hoped that if Alexander were born today, he would be celebrated, not scorned.

Despite all these dramatic life events, Alexander probably would have been forgotten were it not for his greatest achievement: *Cruden's Concordance*. A concordance is essentially an index of the Bible. *Cruden's Concordance* was incredibly detailed, with every word listed with a few words of context and in some cases even including long essays on the subject in question, such as 4,000 words on the history, layout and decoration of synagogues. There are 777,746 words in the Authorised King James Bible; *Cruden's Concordance* has more than two million.

It was a massive undertaking and took him many years to complete. Every day he would go to bed after working as a proof-reader at 1 in the morning – and be up again at 6am to work on his *Concordance*. No one had commissioned him to do this and he had no promise of money waiting for him at the end. It is a task that is impossible to imagine one human taking on by themselves. The first Latin concordance was made by 500 monks. It was less accurate than Cruden's.

Some historians say that this single-minded dedication is a clear sign of Alexander's madness, or joke that if he was not mad when he began his *Concordance*, he must have been by the time he finished it. But Alexander himself saw these Herculean efforts as the way that he could best serve God. Through this, he created a lasting legacy. *Cruden's Concordance* has never been out of print since its publication. According to the *Biographical Dictionary of Eminent Scotsman*, published 86 years after Alexander's death, the *Concordance* is 'so valuable and useful... that it is now reckoned an indispensable part of every clerical library'.

Retrospectively, Alexander has got the credit he deserved. John Betjeman, the then poet laureate, came to Aberdeen in 1968 to unveil a plaque in Cruden's Court, near to where Alexander had been born and which was named after him.

Ultimately, it does not really matter whether Alexander was 'mad'. What we do know is that he was a kind and hardworking person who achieved the seemingly impossible by believing it was possible. It seems a sort of recompense that someone who was shunned and abused throughout his life has eventually achieved such respect from the establishment that his name is woven into the very streets of Aberdeen.

8. SIR COSMO DUFF-GORDON, 5TH BARONET OF HALKIN

Condemned for Escaping the Titanic

1962 - 1931

Some of the people in this book lived perfectly ordinary lives but are remembered for one extraordinary moment. In Sir Cosmo Duff-Gordon's case, it was an episode that would ruin his life and his reputation permanently.

By 1912, Cosmo was reasonably well-known. In Aberdeenshire, people knew him as the 5th Baronet of Halkin and for acting as a Justice of the Peace in Kincardineshire. His reputation on a national scale was based on his fencing career, the peak of which was competing in the Olympics in 1906. Despite his minor celebrity, he was upstaged by his far more famous wife, the divorced Lucy Sutherland, aka Lucile.

Cosmo met Lucy when he became a financial backer for couturiers Maison Lucile. Lucy had launched her own fashion line to support herself and her daughter after her divorce. Like the Parisian Paul Poiret, she favoured less constrictive corsets and low necklines. Lucy claimed to be the first to have live mannequin parades, the forerunners of today's fashion shows. Her success was such that by 1912 she had salons in London, Paris and New York.

Lucy's antics seemed tame by comparison with her sister, the notorious Elinor Glyn, best known for popularising the term 'it' as in 'it girl'. According to Elinor, 'it' meant sex appeal. She wrote both a book and a screenplay called *It* and this success led to her becoming one of Hollywood's earliest female directors. She also gained notoriety for her erotic novel *Three Weeks*, written in 1907.

It was the *Fifty Shades of Grey* of its day and was inspired by Elinor's own affair with an English aristocrat 16 years her junior. Due to one of the sex scenes, it gave rise to a ditty: 'Would you like to sin / With Elinor Glyn / On a tiger skin? / Or would you prefer / To err with her / On some other fur?'

Cosmo's marriage into the family might therefore have been seen as an embarrassing alliance for a respectable baronet. However, far greater scandal was to come, largely as a result of Cosmo's own actions.

Because Lucy needed to visit her New York branch, the couple booked first-class cabins on the Titanic's maiden voyage. It was a decision that Cosmo would come to heartily regret.

The Titanic is famous for having struck an iceberg and sunk, leading to the deaths of around 1,500 passengers and crew. Sir Cosmo became infamous for surviving the Titanic. The couple – along with Lucy's secretary, Laura Francatelli – managed to leave in one of the last lifeboats. Although it had a capacity of 40, there were only 12 people on it. That is in a stark contrast with the very last lifeboat to leave, which had a capacity of 47 but left with 71 people on board.

Because Cosmo was one of the few male passengers to escape and because this was a contravention of the 'women and children first' rule, he was vilified by the press. The Duff-Gordons returned to London to be met by scathing newspaper headlines. Lucy wrote: 'I shall never forget his stricken face when we landed from the RMS Lusitania and caught the boat train for London. All over the station were newspaper placards: "Duff Gordon scandal" ... "Baronet and wife row away from the drowning".' The media claimed that he had bribed his way onto a lifeboat and told the crew of the lifeboat not to return to the ship for any survivors. One newspaper even said that he had dressed as a woman in order to escape.

There was a British Wreck Commissioner's Inquiry into the bribery accusations, looking to establish what happened on that fateful night in the freezing Atlantic Ocean.

Lucy and her secretary Laura were offered places in two previous lifeboats but Lucy refused to leave her husband. In fact, it was her determination to stay with Cosmo that probably saved his life. A little later, they saw the captain's emergency boat being loaded and Cosmo asked whether they could get on board. The officer in charge said he would be glad if they would. They boarded the lifeboat alongside seven crew members and two other passengers.

As they looked back at the disappearing lights on the ship, Lucy said to her secretary, 'There is your beautiful nightdress gone.' One of the members of the crew on board was infuriated at her words; not because she was callously disregarding the hundreds of lives that were lost but because he and the other members of the crew had lost everything. The Duff-Gordons were rich enough to replace their belongings but the staff could not. In fact, their pay would have been stopped the minute that the ship went down.

Perhaps hoping to defuse the situation, Cosmo said that he would pay each of the crew members £5.[10] He wrote them each a cheque on the rescue vessel but some interpreted this gesture as a bribe. Cosmo later said: 'Indeed at that moment I would have given anything that I possessed to anybody who wanted it, as my heart was so full of thanksgiving that the two women in my charge and myself were where we were.'

The British Wreck Commissioner's Inquiry concluded that Cosmo had not bribed the crew in order to prevent the lifeboat from returning to the ship to pick up anyone in the water. However, it added that had Sir Cosmo made the suggestion to go back, the crew probably would have done so and lives would have been saved.

---

[10] The equivalent of around £600 nowadays.

Although cleared by the inquiry of any wrongdoing, Cosmo was broken by the accusations of bribery and cowardice. He became something of a recluse for the rest of his life, spending it at his family estate, Maryculter in Aberdeenshire. Despite the discovery of family letters in 2012 which further vindicated Cosmo of any wrongdoing, his name is forever linked with his escape from the Titanic and an assumption of cowardice. In a deleted scene from the 1997 film *Titanic*, where he was played by Martin Jarvis, he is shown ordering the crew not to return to pick up any survivors. As he put it, 'the whole pleasure of having been saved' was ruined by 'venomous attacks' in the newspapers; these rumours and allegations would follow him for the rest of his days and into the annals of history.

Bonus Bio: Robert Hichens
1882 - 1940

Titanic quartermaster Robert Hichens ended up buried in an Aberdeen graveyard. He was at the wheel when the ship hit the iceberg and managed to escape in one of the lifeboats. In 1940, he was working on a boat off the coast of Aberdeen when he died of heart failure. He is buried in Trinity Cemetery in Aberdeen.

9. DONALD DINNIE

Scotland's Greatest Athlete?

1837 - 1916

Donald Dinnie may have been the greatest athlete that Scotland ever produced. During his 50-year career, he won at least 11,000 contests, including more than 2,000 hammer-throwing competitions and more than 2,000 wrestling matches. Donald also competed in many other events that make up the fare of Highland games, including stone-putting, caber-tossing, running and jumping. He even won prizes for non-sporting contests like Highland dancing and elocution.

He was often described as the 'Strongest Man in the World' or the 'Greatest Athlete in the World', with crowds regularly numbered in their thousands to see him perform. On his first tour of North America, 15,000 people turned up to see him in Toronto. It is estimated that over the course of his career, somewhere between three million to five million spectators saw him perform.

One of the main reasons such a remarkably successful athlete is not more recognised nowadays is down to unfortunate timing. The first modern Olympic Games took place in 1896 when Donald's physical prowess was beginning to decline. If he had competed at the peak of his abilities, he would likely have been an Olympic champion many times over; his sprinting, high jump, weightlifting, shot-put and wrestling records were all superior to the ones of those who took the gold. He might even have picked up a couple of silvers for pole vault, long jump and triple jump.

Donald was born in Balnacraig, near Aboyne, in 1837. Following in his father's footsteps, he became a stonemason and in his free time started competing – and winning – at Highland games. By the age of 33, his fame was so great that Caledonian clubs in the United States and Canada paid for him to come over and compete against their champions. Donald would get a fee as well as any money he won competing. At each gathering, he regularly won between 12 and 16 events, sometimes scooping up prize money of £200 to £300 a day[11], more than the average labourer would earn in a year.

As well as competing, Donald would put on displays of his strength at music halls. He would welcome wrestling and weightlifting challengers and was rarely bested. One of his favourite displays of strength was when he would hold his arm out straight and have a 56 lb (25 kg) weight placed in the palm of his hand. Donald would hold this weight up for at least 25 seconds and sometimes as long as three-quarters of a minute. He offered £1[12] for every second that another man could hold the same weight. Throughout his travels in the United States, Canada, New Zealand, Australia and South Africa, he never had to pay out – nobody could hold a weight for any length of time with the arm out completely straight.

Donald's travels took him away from Scotland for long periods. On one occasion he made a trip to North America and then decided to go to New Zealand and Australia. He did not return to his homeland for 16 years. He would have been back slightly sooner but the steamer he took back from Australia stopped in at Cape Town in South Africa. When his fans learned he was on board, they stormed the ship and demanded that he do a tour of the country.

Donald was an impressive sight. Standing tall at 6ft 1in (1.85m), he performed in tights or a kilt, which was sometimes the only item he was wearing, much to the delight of the women in the crowd. It was said that the

---

[11] Equivalent to £20,000 to £30,000 nowadays.
[12] Approximately £100 nowadays.

proud Scotsman never owned a pair of trousers. He was such an excellent physical specimen that while in Australia he modelled for a statue of William Wallace which was carved for Ballarat Botanical Gardens in Victoria.

It was while in the Antipodes that the passage of time started to creep up on him. In 1896, when he was almost 60 years old, he 'only' competed in three events at a gathering in Auckland – not that old age did anything to lessen his fame. In 1903 he was asked by Robert Barr to endorse his soft drink Iron Brew (now Irn-Bru) and an image of Donald appeared on the bottle, recommending the drink 'to all who wish to aspire to athletic fame'. It perhaps was not the sincerest endorsement since on Donald's first trip to the United States, he was reported to only ever drink milk but perhaps his tastes changed in later life. His image also appeared on cigarette cards and he was a household name, demonstrated by the fact that soldiers in the World War One trenches nicknamed the 16 lb mortar shells 'Donald Dinnies'.

Despite winning prize money of more £25,000[13] over the course of his career, he was on the brink of poverty by his 70s. Throughout his career, he always sent money home but also invested a lot in Australia, much of which was lost during the 1890s economic depression, the worst in all of Australia's history.

To make money, he decided to go back on the stage in London. Part of his act involved holding up a platform while two dancers did a Highland fling on it. Councillors became concerned that he was too old and was putting his safety in danger, and he was subsequently banned from performing. At this point, *Health and Strength* magazine stepped in to fundraise for Donald and ran a benefit night in London, at which the Master of Ceremonies was fellow Scot William Bankier (see profile below).

---

[13] Approximately £2.5 million nowadays.

Donald died in 1916 and such was his global fame and appeal, his death was even reported in the *New York Times*. His legacy lived on, partly through his children. His son Eugene also performed as a strongman and was able to lift a platform with a piano and six men on it. But Donald also gave his name to a tiny bit of the Aberdeenshire landscape which still acts as a challenge to strongmen and women across the world.

Around 1860, Donald picked up two stones, one weighing 318.5 lbs (144.47 kg) and the other 414.5 lbs (188.02 kg), which together equate to the weight of four average men. The stones were located near the Bridge of Potarch over the River Dee, close to Kincardine O'Neil. They had sat there for several decades with iron rings attached to them after they were used to secure scaffolding for bridge repairs. Donald carried them the width of the bridge and back, a distance of 17ft 1.5in (5.2m). Since this feat, the stones have been known as the Dinnie Stones and hundreds of people have journeyed to Aberdeenshire to attempt to lift them. Since Donald managed it, as of 2019, only five people have been able to carry the stones any distance at all and none have been able to carry them as far as he did without stopping.

Bonus Bio: William Bankier aka Apollo, the Scottish Hercules
1870 - 1949

Donald Dinnie is not the only strongman to hail from Aberdeenshire. William Bankier was born in Banff in 1870 and at the age of 12, ran off to join the circus. Although swiftly retrieved by his parents, he eventually got his wish and performed in numerous circuses and roadshows, as a strongman and doing wrestling and boxing. At one point, he worked in Buffalo Bill's Wild West Show. He was best known as Apollo, the Scottish Hercules, and the act he is most famous for involved harness-lifting an adult elephant.

10. GEORGE FINDLATER

'Hero of Dargai' Turned Music Hall Act

1872 - 1942

During the second half of the 19th century, the British Army made 62 military expeditions into the North-West Frontier of British India (now part of Pakistan) to try to control the Pashtun tribes and the border with Afghanistan. The most significant of these was the Tirah Campaign of 1897-98, the greatest threat to the British Empire in the region since the Indian Rebellion of 1857. It took the British almost a year of fighting and the deployment of 63,000 soldiers before they eventually came to terms with the tribes. Analysis after the event suggested that the whole affair could have been avoided if the British had not acted in a way that convinced the tribes that their lands and way of life were about to be colonised.

This was the context in which George Findlater became the 'Hero of Dargai'. Perhaps you could say that the British needed a win. Several months after the tribes had declared war on the British, the army decided on a show of force in Tirah. The North-West Frontier was incredibly mountainous and in order to get an army there, they first had to prepare a road. This gave the tribes a bit of a clue as to what the British planned to do. Afridi and Orakzai tribesmen occupied the Dargai Heights, a place which gave them an uninterrupted view of the road below and a perfect opportunity to fire on the soldiers beneath. Three battalions of Gurkhas, Dorsets and Derbys had already tried to storm the Heights but had been held back by heavy fire. More than 100 soldiers had been killed. Now it was the turn of the 1st

Battalion Gordon Highlanders.[14] The colonel addressed his men: 'The General says this hill must be taken at all costs - the Gordon Highlanders will take it.' The advance was announced.

Traditionally, Highland regiments would be accompanied into battle by pipers who would inspire the men to fight through stirring tunes on the bagpipes. Accordingly, four pipers led the advance across the exposed piece of land. It can hardly have been the most musical of moments: the pipers were ordered to play the regimental march, 'The Cock o' the North', but in the noise and commotion, Piper Findlater missed the command and instead opted to play 'The Haughs o' Cromdale', a pacier Strathspey. Bullets rained down on the advancing soldiers. George Findlater was hit a glancing blow to his left ankle and then the bottom of his chanter was shot off. Three-quarters of the way across, he was shot in his right ankle. He later said it felt like he had been struck with a stick. It was his subsequent actions that won him acclaim across the British Empire. Instead of sheltering behind a rock, he propped himself up against a boulder and continued playing, while the blood flowed out of his ankle, turning his kilt red. After about five minutes, George passed out.

The Highlanders continued with their charge, climbing up the rockface and managing to take the Dargai Heights.

Never mind that some historians believe that the Afridi and Orakzai tribesmen may have retreated simply because they ran out of ammunition, the taking of the Dargai Heights was seen as a splendid act of heroism by the acting battalion and the story of George risking his life by continuing to play captured the public's imagination.

George was invalided back to Britain where he received the Victoria Cross, presented by the Queen herself. He

---

[14] For more information on the founding of Aberdeenshire's local regiment, the Gordon Highlanders, see 16. Jane, Duchess of Gordon.

appeared at the Royal Military Tournament, a military pageant celebrating British fighting achievements. Public subscriptions were set up to supply him with several new sets of pipes. Paintings, poems and songs were created to commemorate the battle. Photographs of George were sold to the public, as were souvenir 'Dargai Cigars'. The most blatant attempt to cash in on the Dargai Heights was probably by sauce company Musgrave & Co, 'Pioneers in Patriotism in sauces', who released a sauce named 'Dargi-Dash', claiming at the time that it 'stimulates Health, Endurance and Courage. Valour and Quality go Hand in Hand.'

Perhaps realising that everyone but himself was profiting from his sudden fame, George decided to take his show on the road. After he had been invalided out of the army, he received an offer to perform at the Alhambra Music Hall in London, where he re-enacted the taking of the Dargai Heights on stage, and for which he was paid 25 guineas a night.[15]

This caused an uproar. George was seen as opportunistically profiting from his Victoria Cross. One newspaper claimed that he was being paid 15 times the salary of the Swiss president, a ridiculous assertion since it was based on George receiving his Alhambra fee every day for an entire year.

Under pressure from the army, the show closed. All the furore over George's music hall career brought the public's attention to the pitifully small pension that former soldiers, even Victoria Cross recipients, received. Questions were asked in Parliament over the army's interference in George's performances and it was claimed that previous Victoria Cross winners had become so impoverished that they ended their days in workhouses.

George was offered a post as the lodge-keeper at Balmoral Castle but turned it down because of the paltry

---

[15] Equivalent to approximately £2,900 nowadays.

pay and because, at 25 years old, he did not fancy a job 'where I might drag through the remainder of my life'. Instead, George toured and performed for a year, including six months in North America.

Although famous for his piping, it is unclear whether George was actually any good at playing them. In September 1898, he entered the bagpipe competitions at the Aberdeen Highland Gathering and failed to place in any of the categories, despite his fame. He had, after all, only taken up the pipes after he enlisted in the 2nd Battalion Gordon Highlanders in 1888, aged 16.

At 27 years old, George settled down and married his cousin, Nellie Findlater. He used the money he had saved from performing to secure the tenancy of a farm in Forglen. George and Nellie had five children and he worked quietly as a farmer until the outbreak of the First World War.

He joined up once again and served until he was wounded at Loos and invalided home. He lived out his days in Forglen in Turriff, a quiet end for a man who had once symbolised everything the British wanted to believe about their empire and the men who fought to uphold it.

11. SIR EWAN FORBES, 11TH BARONET OF CRAIGIEVAR, AND WILLIAM FORBES-SEMPILL, 19TH LORD SEMPILL

Transgender Baronet and his Traitor Brother

1912 - 1991 and 1893 - 1965

Sometimes a normal life can be extraordinary, just as a result of the circumstances around it. Such is the case with Ewan Forbes, Baronet of Craigievar. Ewan was born in September 1912 to the 18th Lord Sempill and his wife Gwendolen at the beautiful Craigievar Castle, their family home. He was christened Elizabeth and brought up as a girl, although, because he was extremely reluctant to go to a girls' boarding school, for the latter part of his education he was home-schooled. He had a season in London as a debutante where he was presented at court. He studied medicine at the University of Aberdeen and became a general practitioner in Alford, Aberdeenshire.

However, in September 1952, a simple announcement appeared in the *Aberdeen Press and Journal* stating: 'Dr. E. Forbes-Sempill, Brux Lodge, Alford wishes to intimate that in future he will be known as Dr. Ewan Forbes-Sempill. All legal formalities have been completed.' At the same time, Ewan applied to the Sheriff Court to have the gender and the first name on his birth certificate changed. This caused something of a stir and the announcement was even picked up by *Time Magazine*. When Ewan was interviewed, he said it had all been the result of a 'ghastly mistake' when he was born, which meant he was 'carelessly registered as a girl', and he blamed the repression of an earlier generation: 'I have been sacrificed to prudery, and the horror which our parents had about sex.'

What is remarkable about all of this is that Ewan's re-registration and change of name seem to have been widely accepted in 1950s Aberdeenshire. It may have helped that Ewan had been presenting as male ever since he moved to Alford and even as a teenager he had always worn trousers or the kilt whenever he could. He said that his patients had been wholly supportive when they heard about the change and he seems to have been held in high esteem by the local community, eventually becoming an elder at the church. A month after the announcement in the paper, his changed birth certificate allowed him to legally marry his housekeeper Isabella Mitchell.

Although Isabella and Ewan came from very different social backgrounds, theirs was a love match. They shared a passion for all things Doric and became pillars of the local community, founding a Scottish country dancing troop, the Dancers of Don. They remained a devoted, and childless, couple until Ewan's death in 1991.

After their wedding, Ewan continued to live the quiet life of a country doctor. But all this was profoundly shaken by the death of his elder brother William in 1965.

Ever since their father's death in 1934, William had been the 10th baronet and 19th Lord Sempill but had left the management of his Fintray and Craigievar estates to Ewan. When William died, the barony and the baronetcy split. The barony passed to the next in the line of succession so went to William's daughter Ann. The baronetcy was only allowed to go to a man and William had no sons. This meant that it passed to William's closest male relation, his brother Ewan. If it had not been for Ewan, the baronetcy would have passed to a cousin, John Forbes-Sempill. This cousin was not pleased to miss out on the baronetcy, along with which went the bulk of the estate and Craigievar Castle. He challenged the legality of the changed birth certificate and a case was brought to the Court of Session to determine to whom the baronetcy should go to by ruling whether Ewan was legally a man or a woman.

It took three years for a decision to be made and during that time Ewan was examined by 12 medical experts, all of whom gave evidence in the case. There was no accepted precedent for what determined gender and many factors were considered, including chromosomes, genitalia and Ewan's psychological state. There had only been one previous gender-determination case in Scotland like this, with Tayside Sheriff Court refusing a birth certificate correction from male to female in 1957.

In Ewan's case, the court concluded that he was a 'hermaphrodite', tending towards the male. That was not the opinion of all the medical experts and it was acknowledged that the tests conducted were not completely reliable. However, the judge ruled in Ewan's favour and he was allowed to keep the baronetcy, as well as his altered birth certificate. Intriguingly, one of the experts later stated that 'psychological sex' was the factor that most influenced the judge's decision, being given more weight than biological evidence.

This case could have created a legal precedent: the courts had decided that it was possible to change the gender on a birth certificate and for that to be legally binding. This should have meant that since the 1960s, transgender and intersex people in Scotland could legally determine their own gender.

Unfortunately, Ewan's case was heard in private, the documents were not publicly filed and, instead of being heard in a court, the case was heard in a solicitor's office. This meant that the legal precedent was instead set by Corbett v Corbett in 1971, a case focusing on the marriage of Arthur Corbett, a cisgender man, and April Ashley, a transgender woman. The court did not accept that April was a woman and thereby created a precedent with international implications: namely that gender could not be changed from the one assigned at birth. This remained the case in the UK until 2004.

However, perhaps even if Ewan's case had been heard more publicly, it would still have become the exception, rather than the rule. Many of the experts called upon in Ewan's case also testified in Corbett v Corbett. It has been suggested that the reason the Forbes-Sempill family was given privacy boiled down to their aristocratic position.

Ewan's older brother, William, also lived something of a charmed life albeit in different circumstances, as he was a traitor and a spy, yet received no punishment.

There was almost a 20-year age gap between Ewan and his older brother. This meant that in the First World War, William was old enough to serve and he became one of the early pilots. The day the Royal Air Force was created, he was transferred to it, a sign of how important he was.

Because of his involvement in early military aviation, he led a trade mission to Japan in 1921 to set up their naval air service. At this time, Japan was officially allied with Britain. This mission led to Japan being supplied with British planes and receiving training from British pilots, while an aircraft factory was also built. It was this groundwork that in some respects laid the foundations for the Japanese attack on Pearl Harbour. At the time, William was awarded the Order of the Rising Sun, third class.[16]

During the 1920s, William continued to lead trade missions to many different countries across the globe. But MI5 discovered that he was being paid to give British aviation secrets to Japan, despite the fact that the countries were no longer allies. In particular, William joined a delegation on a trip to the Blackburn Aircraft factory where he managed to talk his way into a hangar where a secret seaplane was being developed.

---

[16] For another Scot awarded the Order of the Rising Sun, see 3. Thomas Blake Glover.

Although there was concrete evidence against him, the Director of Public Prosecutions decided not to prosecute as a trial would expose the fact that mail going to and from the Japanese Embassy was being intercepted. It is also suggested that the fact that William's father was an aide to King George V may have played a part, as it would have been an embarrassment to have exposed a spy at the heart of the British establishment.

Some scholars think that William was motivated not by Fascist beliefs or a desire for money, but because of his impetuous nature. However, it seems incredibly likely that he held extreme right-wing views because, in the 1930s, he became a member of several Fascist groups, including The Link, which promoted Anglo-German friendship, and the Right Group, which aimed to 'oppose and expose the activities of Organized Jewry', starting by ridding the Conservative Party of any Jewish influence.

Despite these memberships and the fact that William was a known spy, he re-joined the Royal Naval Air Service when the Second World War broke out and was assigned to the Admiralty. This was a position that gave him direct access to Prime Minister Winston Churchill and to information about the newest developments in aircraft. A few months later, MI5 intercepted Japanese messages about payments being made to William. When the allegations were put to him, William denied passing information to the Japanese and said that the payments had stopped at the outbreak of the war. He was allowed to continue in his post and, in 1941, he used this position to bring about the release of Mitsubishi's London manager, Satoru Makahara, who had been arrested as a suspected spy.

At around the same time, Churchill and American President Franklin D. Roosevelt met in person for the first time for secret talks at Placentia Bay. Soon afterwards the Bletchley codebreakers decoded messages from the Japanese Embassy in London to Tokyo. The information was about this top-secret meeting and was described by

Churchill as 'pretty accurate stuff'. The hunt was on to find the spy close to Churchill.

After a month, MI5 came up with the names of two men who might be the source of the leak; one of the names was William's. Churchill gave the order to 'clear him out' and William was given a choice: resign or be sacked. At this, he protested vehemently and when Churchill heard of the ultimatum that had been made to him, he was shocked, saying, 'I had not contemplated Lord Sempill being required to resign his commission, but only to be employed elsewhere in the Admiralty.'

William was duly offered a position in the North of Scotland. It might seem surprising that he was neither sacked nor prosecuted as a spy. This is possibly down to the fact that it would have been a great embarrassment to the Government if it got out that they had allowed a known spy to hold a position which gave him access to such sensitive secret information. Churchill may have also been reluctant to anger a man who was not only a Conservative peer but who had many friends within the Conservative Party.

It seems to be the case that, for good or for ill, the ordinary rules did not apply to the Forbes of Craigievar.

12. MARY GARDEN

Celebrity Opera Singer who Courted Scandal

1874 - 1967

Although not very well-known nowadays, Mary Garden had an outsized reputation in her own time. She was a soprano opera singer and one of the leading celebrities of her day, known for the emotional depth she brought to her parts. Her fame was so great that when the highway to Mount Rushmore in South Dakota was constructed, it was called Mary Garden Way. Her performances were legendary – not just because of her voice, but because of her acting ability. She would regularly do 20 curtain calls at the end of a show, one contract gave her $1,400[17] per performance and her singing so moved the King of Greece that he gave her a pearl necklace, which would be valued at $1.5 million nowadays, on the spot.

Mary also had a high opinion of her own abilities. She said of her career, 'I began at the top, I stayed at the top and I left at the top.' In many ways, that was true.

Her family left Aberdeen for the United States in 1883 when she was nine years old, eventually settling in Chicago. Mary's talent was spotted at a young age and in 1896, at the age of 22, she was sent to Paris by the wealthy Mayer family to improve her singing. But the Mayers became suspicious that Mary was enjoying herself too much on their money and her allowance was stopped in the spring of 1899. She was unable to pay her rent and forced to move into a tiny room in a boarding house, selling her jewellery to survive.

---

[17] Equivalent to $37,700 nowadays.

But one day she had a stroke of luck. That September, she bumped into the soprano Sibyl Sanderson while walking through a park. Sibyl, who had befriended Mary two years previously but had since taken a break from performing, took pity on the girl and invited Mary to live with her. This put Mary at the heart of the Parisian opera scene. Through Sibyl's connections, the following year she got a chance to audition for the Opéra-Comique and got a part in *Carmen,* which would be performed in October. But before that show opened, she heard about a new opera called *Louise,* which was also being performed at the Opéra-Comique. Although Mary was not performing in *Louise*, she learnt the entire score and went along to the rehearsals.

In April, the main singer developed a severe cold and the understudy was sick. Mary was asked by the venue's manager to come to the performance in full costume and sit in the audience, ready to take over if needed. The lead had to stop halfway through the show and Mary was rushed on stage. Her performance was a triumph and the very next day she was offered a full-time contract for two years. Shortly after that, she took over the leading role in *Louise* permanently. Even at this stage in her career, she was so confident in herself and her position that when she did not like the next opera she was cast in, she refused to turn up for rehearsals.

Her dramatics did at times get her in trouble though. At an event in New York 10 years later, she encountered the Mayers but instead of speaking with her former backers, she snubbed them. The next day, she received notice that they were suing her for $20,000[18] – the original amount they had spent on her, plus interest. Even though by this point she was at the top of her profession, Mary only had $10,000 worth of savings. Fortunately, the president of the bank was an avid opera fan and Mary got her loan. She loved being

---

[18] Equivalent to $396,000 nowadays

able to cut ties with the Mayers once and for all: 'I was flat broke but I was the happiest girl in New York.'

It was one of many profligate moments. On one occasion, her chauffeur was fined for speeding and could not pay the $50 bail. Mary did not have that sum on her either – so she took off her $1,200 diamond bracelet and put it up as security.

As well as a reputation for extravagance, Mary cultivated her image as a scarlet woman. She loved to court the attention of the press by spreading rumours or hinting at a salacious past. Although she was never married, Mary regularly suggested that she might, saying that she was engaged on more than one occasion; one time to a Russian prince, another time to a Sheikh. In 1910, Mary declared that she would write her memoirs about the last 10 years. She was asked if she was going to write about her love affairs. Her response: 'Good gracious, no! Do you think I am going to write volumes?'

One of Mary's most notorious performances was the starring role in *Salome*, a part which involved the dance of the seven veils. By today's standards, it would not be considered particularly scandalous but at the time it caused 'Salomania'. Mary removed the seven veils one-by-one, eventually left standing in front of the audience in nothing more than a small flesh-coloured piece of silk. At its New York debut in 1909, the stunned audience sat in silence a full 30 seconds after the show had ended. In Chicago, the show had to be called off after objections by the Chief of Police, who said Mary 'wallowed around like a cat in a bed of catnip'.

However, the opera proved extremely popular in some quarters. Later in life, Mary attributed her career success to American women who dragged their husbands along to the opera. She said that when the husbands saw her cavorting about onstage with very little on, they took the opera glasses away from their wives and refused to give them back.

Although this may have been a tongue-in-cheek comment, Mary certainly was aware of the importance of capitalising on her sex appeal. In the 1950s, she was coaching a soprano and took the young woman to Paris's red-light district, where they sat in a bar and watched the prostitutes. She told her pupil: 'Watch what they do. How they handle their breasts, touch themselves. Everything is there. They know the value of their sexuality.'

Her flamboyant behaviour did not mean that she could not act with compassion and courage. During the First World War, she helped to fund a hospital in Paris for soldiers wounded in the head or eyes and she herself became a Red Cross nurse. She also tried to join the French army dressed as a man, motivated by her love of France and all the country had done for her. When revealed to be a woman, she said, 'I am sure that I could fight as well as any man if they would only let me. I have never failed to subdue every man that I have met so far.'

But when the Nazis invaded Paris during the Second World War, she returned to Aberdeen, living on Belgrave Terrace. Nowadays, there is a garden in her honour nearby on Craggie Loanings. Despite living abroad for much of her life, she renewed her connection with her Scottish roots long before her permanent return. During a shooting holiday in 1912, she went to a ball where the guests danced until dawn, finishing only when breakfast arrived. 'When the bacon and porridge were finally served, all the men poured stout instead of milk over their porridge and some of them poured it over their bacon too. In that moment I rediscovered Scotland all over again,' she recounted.

In later life, she struggled with dementia. When she died aged 83, she had a mere £2 in the bank and the pearls she always wore turned out to be paste copies. The real ones given her by the King of Greece must have been spent somewhere along the way – no one knows where but, given how Mary lived, it was probably in some extravagant fashion.

13. SHEILA GARVIE AND BRIAN TEVENDALE

Sex, Drugs and Murder

1934 - 2014 and 1945 - 2003

For 10 days in 1968, Aberdeen High Court became the focus of the national press. The queues to get into the public benches were so long that people would bring flasks of soup to keep them warm while they waited. On the last day of the trial, 2 December 1968, they started queueing at 3.30am.

It was, of course, a murder trial that had grabbed the public's imagination. But not just any murder trial. The victim was the young, rich and handsome Maxwell Garvie. In the dock was his wife Sheila, her lover Brian Tevendale and his friend Alan Peters.

From the start, this case had promised salacious details. Max's missing-person profile in the Police Gazette focused on his high-living lifestyle, describing his drinking and use of tranquilliser drugs. It added that he was 'fond of female company but has strong homosexual tendencies and is often in the company of young men'.

The police initially thought Max had gone abroad and only discovered he had been murdered thanks to a tip-off from his mother-in-law. Sheila confessed to her mother that her boyfriend, Brian, had killed her husband. Mrs Watson kept the secret for months but grew concerned about Sheila's continued relationship with Brian. She went to the police and they brought the lovers in for questioning. Eventually, Brian cracked under the pressure of the all-night interrogation. He directed the police to the drains of Lauriston Castle in St Cyrus, where Brian lived. In this tunnel, they found the decomposing corpse of Max Garvie.

During the trial, it emerged that the Garvies' idyllic family life was more unconventional than it at first appeared. On the surface, they were a happily married couple with three children. It had been a Cinderella story for Sheila, who had grown up on the Balmoral estate, with her father earning low wages as the estate mason. By contrast, Max Garvie was a very wealthy farmer; his neighbours called him 'The Flying Farmer' because of his private plane. Sheila and Max lived in the Mearns, an area of Aberdeenshire known for its rich agricultural land.

Max used his wealth to indulge in his other interests. He was a member of several nudist camps and decided to set up his own one in the North East of Scotland. In 1964, he bought a holiday home near Alford and turned it into a nudist colony, nicknamed 'Kinky Cottage' by the locals. They must have had their suspicions about what was going on behind a strategically planted belt of trees and bushes. Former Sunday School teacher Sheila was not interested and said that she would be far happier looking after the children. But, as the court was told, Max put pressure on her to join in.

He next decided to convince Sheila to try swinging. Max was an office bearer for the Scottish National Party and through the party, he met Brian Tevendale. He decided that the handsome 20-year-old mechanic would be the perfect 'toy boy' for 31-year-old Sheila. He took to inviting Brian to their house, leaving Brian and Sheila alone together and afterwards questioning her about whether they had slept together yet. The whole idea of having sex with someone other than her husband upset Sheila. But eventually, Max brought them together by forcing a naked Sheila into Brian's room in the middle of the night.

Max also started an affair – with Brian's sister, Trudi Birse, the respectable wife of an Aberdonian policeman. In the witness box, Trudi described Max's sexual appetites and how they had had sex in the cockpit of his plane as they flew over the North East. On the nights when Trudi was unavailable, Brian would be invited round to the Garvies' mansion, where Brian and Max would toss a coin to decide who slept with Sheila. After Max lost the coin toss a couple of times, he changed the rules so that they would all three go to bed together.

Far from enjoying the life of swinging and affairs that Max had introduced her to, Sheila's memoir describes an abusive relationship. After she temporarily left him for Brian, she said Max threatened to kill her, to send her to a mental hospital and almost broke her shoulder. Sheila detailed how Max made her sleep with him after she had had sex with Brian. She also said that from then on, having sex with Max felt like 'being raped by a stranger'. When Sheila described the threesome with Max and Brian, she said: 'I felt like an object being passed around from one to another. I lost all respect for myself and felt utterly degraded.'

A part of the book that really sticks out is when Sheila tries to leave her husband. The advice that she gets from almost everyone, including her parents, is to return to her husband for the sake of the children. She writes: 'If my husband had been a postman or a farm labourer, everyone would have said "Leave him! Get out!" But Max was a powerful man in the community, popular and with a great deal of influence, and everyone was on his side...I wasn't married to a postman or a farm labourer. I was married to the mighty Max Garvie – so therefore everything must be all right and I was just being a silly woman.'

This is, of course, not to say that Max deserved to be murdered. In this case, history has been written by those who survived it. There has been no one to stand up and defend Max Garvie, with the possible exception of his eldest daughter, Wendy. In a newspaper interview in 2002, she said: 'My father was painted as a manipulating monster, but as we all know, nothing is ever that black and white. I wonder now just how much of it all was truth.'

Certainly, some parts of Sheila's memoir are striking for the strict morality attached to sex. One wonders if the black way Max is portrayed is affected by this. There is a homophobic undercurrent, most notable when she talks about the 'problem' of lesbianism in women's prisons. When she discusses Max's homosexuality, she uses the words 'odd' and 'strange', and she makes it clear that she saw Max's sexual desires as 'unnatural'.

Just as we will never know exactly what the Garvies' marriage was like, we will never know what really happened the night that Max was murdered. Sheila and Brian made very different statements about what had happened.

Brian said that Sheila had let him and Alan into the house, served them drinks and handed him the rifle with which he was to kill her husband. It was a story he stuck to in his last interview in 1999 when he stated that Sheila had been the driving force behind the murder and described himself as being 'under her spell'.

Sheila said that she had been woken up by Brian and his friend Alan and been ushered into the bathroom. After a while, she claims she was let out and told: 'He won't worry you anymore.' It was then that she discovered her husband was dead. In her memoir, written 18 months after she was released from prison, Sheila maintained that she had nothing to do with her husband's death. She wrote: 'I had no hand in my husband's murder, but I deserved my sentence because I failed to halt the tide of events which led inexorably to his death.'

Despite these conflicting versions of events, Sheila and Brian were both found guilty and given life sentences.[19]

Even though Brian's statement to the police was used as evidence against her, Sheila declared her love for Brian from the dock. The newspapers described how, when the verdict

---

[19] Alan Peters was found 'not proven'. This is a verdict only available in the Scottish courts and it has the same result as not guilty.

was handed down, they kissed before being led away separately. They were sent to different prisons and Brian sought permission from the Secretary of State to get married. But three months into their sentences, Sheila sent Brian a letter in which she said, 'I have decided to have nothing more to do with you ever again.' Brian later speculated that this was because she had been prevented from seeing her children. Sheila's lawyer Lawrence Dowdall wrote that her affection for Brian was tested by the fact that he had not testified in court that she had nothing to do with the murder. He adds that Sheila's feelings for Brian were completely killed when she heard that he was negotiating to sell her love letters to a Sunday newspaper.

After 10 years, they were both released from prison. Sheila took over the running of her aunt's bed and breakfast in Aberdeen. Brian became a pub landlord in Perthshire. The authorities encouraged them not to see each other again but in her memoir, the recently released Sheila hoped to rectify that: 'I felt – and still feel – that for us not to meet again after all that happened is rather like a story without an ending.'

Brian's last words on the matter 19 years later were quite different: 'I can't say I feel anything about her now. She has her life to get on with and so do I.'

They married other people. In fact, Sheila married twice more, firstly to Rhodesian-born welder David McLellan in 1979. Shortly after her divorce from McLellan two years later, she married drilling engineer Charles Mitchell and they are reported to have lived happily together until he died in 1992. Brian died in 2003 and Sheila in 2014. Despite Sheila's hope that they would meet again, it never happened, with the last time the lovers saw each other being the day they were sentenced for the murder of Sheila's husband.

14. BILL GIBB

Fashion Designer who Never Forgot his Roots

1943 - 1988

'My knight in shining armour,' was how model and 1960s icon Twiggy described Bill Gibb after he helped rescue her purple Mini from a snowdrift. It was their first meeting and the beginning of a friendship. But it was also an appropriate description for a man who would go on to design the luxurious dresses she wore to the various premieres of her 1971 film *The Boy Friend,* which made her 'feel like a princess'. It was also a rather fitting description for a man who, ever since boyhood, had been fascinated by historical clothes and persuaded his three sisters to dress up as people from history, using bedspreads and curtains, and arrange them in visually arresting tableaux.

From an early age, Bill's talent was recognised. Growing up in a family of farmers near New Pitsligo, he was always designing clothes and drawing historical dress details in his school jotters. Even when he became a famous fashion designer, he remained proud of his farming background and close to his family, inviting them to all his London fashion shows and regularly visiting the farm with celebrity friends like Twiggy in tow. His family were incredibly proud of him and always encouraged him to succeed, even from an early age: his grandmother inspired him with her own landscape portraits and by letting him dress her up; his mother encouraged him to enter a dress design competition through the Women's Rural Institute - which he won - when Bill was aged 15; and his aunt took him to interview at the prestigious St Martin's School of Art in London for a place on their fashion course. Bill was so nervous that he was hardly able to get out a word and his aunt had to speak up for him, saying that although he was not able to talk, he was talented.

Bill got in. Before he left for London, he told his mother that if he had not made it by the time of his 30th birthday, he would be back to drive the tractor. In fact, Bill wanted to come home a lot sooner. He became homesick and struggled with sewing and the fact that many people did not understand his accent. His parents persuaded him to persevere and he graduated top of his class and got a scholarship to the Royal College of Art (RCA), where his contemporaries included future fashion designers Ossie Clark and Zandra Rhodes. In his memory, his family later set up a scholarship to the RCA in his name, one of the beneficiaries of which was Christopher Bailey, who went on to lead fashion house Burberry.

However, it was a chance meeting in a nightclub with American artist Kaffe Fassett which was to have a transformative impact on the rest of his life. The two of them became partners and artistic collaborators. They went on a three-month trip across the United States, taking inspiration from everything they saw. Kaffe started knitting, coming up with unusual patterns and striking colours. Bill would integrate these designs into his clothes in unconventional ways.

Two years after dropping out of the RCA, Bill was *Vogue*'s Designer of the Year. Incredibly, this was despite not having set up his own fashion label; he was currently working as a freelance designer for mass-market fashion house Baccarat. *Vogue* decided to feature him in the magazine purely based on his sketches. In order to do a fashion shoot, they had to persuade Baccarat to make up some of the designs and even made a few in-house themselves. The resulting shoot was featured simultaneously in British *Vogue*, American *Vogue* and *The Sunday Times*. It caused an immediate sensation. *Vogue* described Bill's style as 'fashion anarchy' and his mixture of patterns and textures, as well as his emphasis on personal expression, went on to define 1970s fashion.

By the time he had his first fashion show, he was an industry name and the elite of the fashion world turned out to see it, including fashion photographers Cecil Beaton and David Bailey and model Grace Coddington. Despite this, he did not forget his Aberdeenshire roots and that same year, even though he was one of the most in-demand designers in London, he held a fashion show at the Royal Darroch Hotel in Cults - although his avant-garde style seems to have left the ladies of Aberdeen a little confused.

His emphasis on colour and luxury made him a designer of choice for the celebrities of the day and he dressed such stars as Bianca Jagger, Cilla Black and Rod Stewart. He would regularly provide clothes to Elizabeth Taylor; in 1976, she wore one of his dresses to the British Film Awards and much to his amusement he saw on TV that she had worn it back-to-front to better show off her cleavage.

Bill's designs were also popular in the mainstream, even if his clothes were beyond the budget of most people. He did numerous collaborations with magazines where they would release a Bill Gibb knitting pattern for their readers; these would regularly bring in £250,000 of additional sales for the magazines.

Bill's signature was a bumble bee, which appeared on all of his clothes and designs until 1985, based on a bumble bee brooch Kaffe had designed for him. The bee might appear as little buttons on a coat or as part of some elaborate embroidery. Sometimes it was squat and round, sometimes elongated and elegant.

Because of the slightly fantastical nature of his creations, he was in hot demand as a wedding dress designer, providing dresses for the singer Lulu and actress Tessa Dahl. Again, this enthusiasm for Bill Gibb creations was mimicked in the mainstream, with the *Daily Mirror* offering a Bill Gibb wedding dress as a prize for their Bride of the Year. He also designed the wedding dresses for his three sisters, although this caused some creative conflict among the siblings. Bill insisted that the wedding dresses should have trains but his sisters argued the aisle of the local church was not long enough. As he had done when they were children, Bill got his way.

The wedding dress for his sister Patsy was particularly stressful. Bill still had not finished the dress the night before the wedding. When the dress was eventually completed, his Italian pattern cutter insisted that it needed some horse's hair sewn in for luck. Accordingly, Bill's father went out and cut some hair off a farm horse which was hastily sewn into the dress on the morning of the wedding. Patsy later remarked that it had worked well: she had been happily married 30 years and counting.

To celebrate 10 years as a designer, the Royal Albert Hall was booked for a fashion retrospective. The 7,000-seater venue sold out. It was a four-and-a-half-hour extravaganza with many celebrities modelling their own Bill Gibb dresses on stage. It proved to be the peak of Bill's career – but few could have anticipated how soon his star would begin to fall.

Less than six months later, Bill's label had to be bailed out. His new backers, property investors the Foxes, insisted that he spend less time on expensive haute couture and focus on ready-to-wear items. Bill's heart was not in it and the partnership lasted only a year. From then on, he ran a smaller operation, making dresses to order and attempting to keep costs down.

Bill struggled with the advent of power-dressing and punk, neither of which really fitted with Bill's luxurious, elaborate, expressive designs. He was not helped by a financial recession or by the fact that *Vogue* stopped covering him. In 1985, he held his first catwalk show in years, inspired by current street fashion and called Bronze Age. It was a great departure from his signature style and, as an acknowledgement of that, it was his first collection in more than a decade to have no bees. Intended to be his great comeback, the collection received few orders. Less than three years later, he died of colon cancer.

Fashion observers have said that although he had a genius for creating clothes, he did not have a head for business or finance and that was his downfall. It is not surprising that he was not interested in the financial side of things. He was far more concerned with beauty than with material objects. In an interview he did in 1976, he told the reporter that all his possessions would fit into one bag and there were only four things he really cherished: two chemist chests, a 1930s porcelain head and his bee collection. He also said how he was currently between homes and sleeping on a friend's sofa – this despite the fact that he was at the height of his popularity and fame.

Perhaps surprisingly for a fashion designer, he did not spend much on his own attire, preferring to buy second-hand clothes and rework them in unusual ways, turning a t-shirt into a hat or pairing a policewoman's coat with some straw sandals.

Although his name has since fallen out of the mainstream, his influence lives on, with people like Giles Deacon, John Galliano and Vivienne Westwood all citing him as one of their favourite designers.

One of his last projects before his death was a book called *Hollywood Knits*, made up of knitting patterns that recreated famous jumpers worn by the stars. Bill's sister Janet knitted one of the cardigans from the book and went down to London to see him while he was struggling with his illness. Aiming for perfection to the very end, he told her she had put the wrong sort of buttons on it.

15. DR ALEXANDER GORDON

The Original Saviour of Mothers

1752 - 1799

In the first half of the 19th century, the death rate across Europe in women giving birth was five in 1,000. But in hospitals, this could be as much as 10 times higher. For context, nowadays in Britain, the maternal death rate is just nine per 100,000.

A major cause of death in childbirth was something called puerperal fever or childbirth fever. This is a form of sepsis caused by bacteria (usually *Streptococcus pyogenes*) which is transferred into the uterus during or after the birth, often through contact with the attending doctor or midwife. Patients who contracted this would develop a fever, brought on by a severe chill and experience great pain in the lower abdomen. By the fifth day, at least two-thirds of patients would be dead.

The problem was that the medical profession was still relatively clueless about the transferral of disease. Sicknesses were often attributed to miasmas or bad smells while discoveries about bacteria were decades away. Doctors did not see any need to wash their hands between patients. One Scottish doctor, William Campbell, recalled how he had dissected the body of a patient who had died from childbirth fever, removed her uterus without gloves and put it in the pocket of his coat so he could show it to his students later. He neither washed his hands or changed his clothes but went to attend to two more births – and unsurprisingly both of the mothers subsequently died of childbirth fever.

Dr Alexander Gordon was the first to make the connection between the spread of the infection and the actions of the medical staff. Alexander was working at the Aberdeen Dispensary during two epidemics of childbirth fever in 1789 and 1792. Although he had started his career as a surgeon in the Royal Navy, his main interest was in midwifery and obstetrics and he gave lectures on the subject at Marischal College, Aberdeen.

Alexander was a big believer in evidence-based medicine. His notes on the patients, which included details such as who had attended them and when, allowed him to show that medical practitioners were spreading disease. In *A Treatise on the Epidemic Puerperal Fever of Aberdeen in 1795*, he presented the statistics and argued that the epidemic could not have been caused by 'a noxious constitution of the atmosphere' as the disease 'seized such women only as were visited, or delivered, by a practitioner or taken care of by a nurse who had previously attended patients affected by the disease'.

He did not hide away from the fact that he was one of the doctors who had, inadvertently, caused the deaths of his patients through poor hygiene. In his *Treatise,* he openly admitted: 'It is a disagreeable declaration for me to mention that I myself was the means of carrying the infection to a great number of women.'

Although Alexander's ideas of what exactly was causing this disease at a biological level remained somewhat hazy (he spoke about an 'atmosphere of infection' surrounding the doctors and midwives who had attended the sick patients), he had a clear idea of how to deal with it. As well as handwashing, medics were to change any contaminated clothing and rooms were to be thoroughly fumigated between patients. He attributed his reduced mortality rate to these measures. During the 1795 epidemic, 49 out of his 77 patients with childbirth fever survived, meaning that his mortality rate was down to 36%, a significant improvement on what most doctors were achieving at the time. If he had not also bled his patients, perhaps his mortality rate would have been even lower.

Unfortunately, Alexander's success was short-lived. It was accepted practice at the time to give the names of those patients and medical attendants described in the study. The latter group did not appreciate the fact that they were being blamed for the deaths of their patients. His colleagues, particularly the midwives, did all that they could to discredit Alexander's reputation and emphasise the deaths that he was responsible for.

Soon after the *Treatise* was published, Alexander was recalled to serve in the Navy. Tellingly, when he left Aberdeen, he donated several books to the Medical Society of Aberdeen, including eight on obstetrics. Perhaps Alexander knew that he had given up that speciality forever. He served in the Navy for three-and-a-half years, but he contracted tuberculosis and left on half-pay in August 1799, dying at his twin brother's farm in Logie less than two months later.

But despite his untimely demise, he proved to be a man well ahead of his time as fellow doctors unknowingly promoted his ideas, leading to a change in the way medicine was practised around the world.

In 1847, Dr Ignaz Semmelweis was working at the Vienna General Hospital's maternity ward when he found that by introducing handwashing into his ward, he could dramatically reduce the death rate. He became a passionate advocate of handwashing and is described as both the 'father of infection control' and the 'saviour of mothers'.

The point here is not that Alexander made the same discovery some 50 years before Semmelweis. Their parallel experience is more important: both men struggled to convince their colleagues of the necessity of handwashing and hygiene. Professional pride got in the way of medical advances and it was not until the 1860s, when both Semmelweis and Alexander were dead, that Louis Pasteur was able to prove germ theory. The tragedy is that thousands, if not tens of thousands, of lives might have been saved if the evidence that these men provided had been properly considered rather than dismissed out of hand.

16. JANE, DUCHESS OF GORDON

Recruiting a Thousand Men with a Kiss

c. 1748 - 1812

Jane, Duchess of Gordon, was not born in Aberdeen. She did not live here and she did not die here. However, she merits inclusion in this book because she helped to establish the 100th Regiment of Foot, later to become the Gordon Highlanders, Aberdeen's local regiment until 1994. The Gordon Highlanders had a reputation for extraordinary courage, leading Winston Churchill to call them 'the finest regiment in the world'.[20]

The 100th Regiment of Foot was raised in 1794 by the 4th Duke of Gordon and his wife Jane – though she was the one who did all the recruiting. She travelled all around the north of Scotland to enlist men to fight against France. She promised to kiss any man who agreed to join the army. In those days when you enlisted, you accepted an up-front payment, known as the King's shilling. Jane put this payment between her lips and in that way gave it to her recruits.

There is a story that a blacksmith who had already refused to join many other regiments, kissed Jane and then threw the coin into the crowd to show that he was not motivated by money. There are other tales of farmers who accepted the kiss and immediately paid the one-pound fine to withdraw enlistment. They said that a kiss from Jane was worth a pound.

---

[20] For an example of the sort of behaviour that inspired Churchill, check out 10. George Findlater.

In total, she recruited 940 men. She was 45 years old at the time. On 24 June 1794, the 100th Regiment of Foot paraded through Aberdeen for the first time. The new regiment was reviewed in Hyde Park by the King himself, the first time a Highland Regiment had been seen in London since before the 1745 Jacobite Rising.

As well as her military involvement, Jane also had a great political influence. At this point in British politics, there were two main political parties: the Whigs and the Tories. Generally speaking, the Whigs represented the interests of the urban bourgeoisie; the Tories were largely supported by the gentry. Famously, Georgiana, Duchess of Devonshire, was a great entertainer and political hostess for the Whig party. Her Tory equivalent was Jane, who would hold massive parties and entertain on a lavish scale. Notable examples included having 100 people sit down for dinner or inviting guests to stay at Gordon Castle for three months.

Jane was almost like the Tory Chief Whip, making sure that rebellious Members of Parliament stayed in line. Her political influence was such that she got involved with the major issues of the day, like the Regency Crisis of 1789 or the Prince of Wales' debts; in the latter instance, she helped to smooth the way for him to receive money from Parliament which he used to begin work on the Brighton Pavilion.

It was not just her beauty that helped her in the traditional male spheres of politics and the military. She was known as the cleverest women of her day, thanks to her ready wit and adroit manipulation of others. She used this to make good matches for all five of her daughters, scoring three dukes and a Marquis. Jane was skilful at adapting to the situation that she faced. Her youngest daughter Georgiana was on the cusp of being engaged to the Duke of Bedford. Unfortunately, he dropped dead before they could be wed. Jane, knowing that her daughter looked particularly good in black, bade her put on widow's weeds and summoned the new Duke of Bedford to comfort his brother's erstwhile almost-fiancée. Soon the young pair were married.

Despite all Jane's manoeuvring, Henry Dundas thwarted her intention to marry her eldest daughter to the Prime Minister of the day, William Pitt the Younger. But her barbed wit put Dundas in his place when she was leaving a party: 'Mr Dundas, you are used to speak in public; will you call my servant?'

Jane also helped to popularise many things that we think of as integral to Scottish identity nowadays. She wore tartan at a time when it was still illegal and promoted Scottish country dancing by insisting her guests dance reels and strathspeys. When she was living in Edinburgh, she would hold literary soirees. It was here that Robert Burns first performed his poetry to the upper echelons of Edinburgh society.

She was able to achieve all of this because of her social position: the wife of the 4th Duke of Gordon. It had been rather a winding path to that marriage. Jane spent her teenage years in Edinburgh where her family had a flat off the High Street. At the age of 14, she was out playing on the Royal Mile when her finger got caught in the wheel of a cart. The cart moved off with her finger still stuck, ripping it off her hand. She was ashamed of this physical impairment and tried to hide it throughout her life, wearing gloves with a wooden finger in place of the missing one.

But she was still considered a noted beauty, given the nickname 'the flower of Galloway'. At the age of 16, she fell in love with a young army officer called Captain Fraser. Unfortunately, he was sent overseas and she soon received word he was dead. The heartbroken Jane accepted the marriage proposal of Alexander, 4th Duke of Gordon, her next-door neighbour in Edinburgh. The story goes that while she and her new husband were on honeymoon in Berwickshire, she received a letter. It was from Captain Fraser saying that he had been wrongly reported as dead and asking for her hand in marriage. It was such a shock that she fainted, only to be found by her new husband who read the letter himself.

There is some evidence that Jane and Captain Fraser managed to reunite. Jane had great difficulty marrying off her fourth daughter, Louisa. A marriage was arranged between Louisa and Lord Brome but his father objected to the match. He didn't want his son to marry a daughter of the Duke of Gordon because there were rumours of madness in the Gordon bloodline. Jane took the direct approach, telling him not to worry 'as there is not a drop of Gordon blood in Louisa's body'. The marriage went ahead.

For his part, the Duke of Gordon was just as unfaithful to his wife. His mistress gave birth to a son at around the same time Jane did. Both boys were named George. Jane distinguished between the two children with the same name by referring to 'my George and the Duke's George'.

Perhaps unsurprisingly, in later life the couple were estranged. Although he agreed to support her financially, he was running out of money and Jane spent the last few years of her life moving from hotel to hotel. She died in Pulteney's Hotel in Piccadilly. It is said that the waiters made a fortune displaying her body to members of the public anxious to see the famous Duchess. Even in death, Jane could still cause a stir.

17. ISHBEL HAMILTON-GORDON, LADY ABERDEEN

Politico who Made her Mark on Both Sides of the Atlantic

1857 - 1939

In 19th-century Britain, women had very little political influence. Although her power was initially acquired through her husband's position, Ishbel Hamilton-Gordon was the exception. Ultimately, she had far more political sway than him, all thanks to her determination and sense of duty.

As a young woman, Ishbel was rather shy and described by her contemporaries as fat. This certainly would have made it harder to make a good marriage, as was the duty of all upper-class girls at the time. But through perseverance, she managed to marry a man who not only gave her a platform for her philanthropy but whom she was – at least initially – also deeply in love with.

Ishbel met John Hamilton-Gordon four years before she officially 'came out' as a debutante in London society. When riding in the park, his friend had gone off with her sister, leaving John to make awkward conversation with the 14-year-old girl who was 10 years his junior. She had been besotted with him ever since.

John had become the 7th Earl of Aberdeen through rather unusual circumstances. He had two elder brothers, one of which shot himself at Cambridge University and the other who ran away to become a sailor and drowned. This unlikely combination of events led to John inheriting the title aged just 23 years old.

After Ishbel came out in 1875, John was a frequent dinner guest at her parents' house. London society fully suspected that it was only a matter of time before he proposed. Gossip reached a head when Queen Victoria despatched her lady-in-waiting to find out whether the rumours were true.

But the months came and went. After two years, John decided that he had to make his intentions clear – he had a meeting with Ishbel's mother in which he told her that he felt only friendship for her daughter. Ishbel was devastated, writing in her diary: 'The one dream of my life for the past six years has dissolved into nothing and I must face life without him.'

However, Ishbel's mother was not about to give in without a fight. She sent a letter after the young Earl, hotly rebuking him for having led them on. John was deeply affected by this and wrote a response saying that he had changed his mind and asking for permission to call. As soon as he had posted it, he regretted his decision, attempting to fish it out of the post box and even trying to get in touch with the postmaster general. It was too late; the letter was sent. A week later, he proposed marriage to Ishbel.

Despite this inauspicious beginning and Ishbel's later affair with Henry Drummond[21], their marriage appears to have been largely happy. Their similarity of beliefs was demonstrated on their honeymoon in Egypt. They heard rumours that slaves were readily available in the country and wanted to see if this was true. They told the captain of their ship that they were interested in buying slaves. Shortly afterwards, four boys, between the ages of eight and 16, were presented to them. The Aberdeens found out that they had been kidnapped from Sudan. John pointed to the Union

---

[21] Ishbel is believed to have had a relationship with the theologian and author Henry Drummond in the 1880s and some suspect that her youngest (and favourite) son, Ian Archibald, was his child.

Jack flying atop the ship and declared the boys free. They were sent to a Presbyterian mission school in Egypt. Two of the boys died, although one of them did use his education to later become a teacher in his homeland's capital, Khartoum.

Once they returned to Haddo Estate in Aberdeenshire, Ishbel turned her attention to the typical activities of upper-class women: childbearing and interior design. But she was unusual in that she was greatly interested in the lives of her many servants and sought to improve them. She started a Household Club which all the servants were invited to join. It included social evenings as well as various classes, such as singing lessons led by the head forester and a carving class taught by the governess. She also put on dances and holiday meals for the staff, something so uncommon that once again rumours were swirling around the Aberdeens. Queen Victoria herself wanted to find out whether the scandalous gossip was true: did the family really eat with their servants?

In neighbouring villages, Ishbel set up a country hospital, a training institute and a programme of hot penny lunches for schoolchildren. On a national scale, she established the Onward and Upward Association, which provided correspondence courses for servant girls in every subject from geography and literature to knitting and bible studies. This grew to include some 8,280 members across Scotland.

Meanwhile, Ishbel was working hard on her husband to convince him to switch political allegiance from the Conservatives to the Liberals. She succeeded and, as a reward for supporting him through a couple of elections, Prime Minister William Gladstone made John the Viceroy of Ireland in 1886. It was a dangerous time to be a representative of the British Government in Ireland. Just four years earlier, the Chief Secretary of Ireland and the Permanent Undersecretary had been assassinated in broad daylight in Phoenix Park in Dublin.

Despite this, Ishbel threw herself into her new role. She was an ardent supporter of Home Rule for Ireland and the Aberdeens were a popular young couple, particularly as Ishbel sought to relieve famine and stimulate industrial growth in Ireland. She became an ambassador for Irish textiles, particularly hand-woven lace. However, the Home Rule Bill was defeated six months later and the Aberdeens were recalled from Ireland in what felt like a great blow to the Irish nationalist movement.

After the Liberals were voted back into office in 1892, Gladstone told John that he could have any viceregal post that he wanted – except Ireland. In the years that had passed since the bill's defeat, Home Rule had split the Liberal Party and, because Ishbel was so closely associated with Home Rule, it would be too politically contentious to send the Aberdeens to Ireland again.

John opted to become Governor-General of Canada. Once there, Ishbel became involved in Canadian politics, working behind the scenes to determine the new Prime Minister. She became the first women to address the Canadian House of Commons and the first woman to receive an honorary degree. She established the National Council of Women, to bring together like-minded ladies to campaign on a variety of issues, in conjunction with her work as President of the International Council of Women (ICW).

Perhaps most significantly, she set up the Victorian Order of Nurses (VON) to provide medical attention to remote communities. This was at first hotly protested by Canadian doctors who worried that the standard of healthcare might drop – and that they might lose out financially if people looked to nurses rather than doctors to provide healthcare. But Ishbel eventually won them over. The VON is still going to this day and has a staff numbering more than 5,000.

Eventually, Ishbel got her wish and, in 1906, John became Viceroy of Ireland once again. They hoped to be the last viceregal couple, overseeing a period of transition to Home Rule. It was not to be. Their second term in Ireland lasted until 1915 when they were recalled for not showing enough enthusiasm for the war effort. Perhaps if they had been allowed to stay, they might have had a moderating effect on Ireland's nationalist movement and the separation from Britain might not have created such a lasting legacy of conflict. Or maybe that is just wishful thinking. By the time the Aberdeens were back in office in 1906, attitudes to Britain had hardened significantly and there was a lot less faith in Home Rule.

That is not to say that the Aberdeens' time in Ireland was of no use. Ishbel directed her attention towards housing and health reform, something that was greatly needed: in Dublin, there was extreme poverty and more than one-fifth of families lived in only one room. In 1907, the death rate from TB in Ireland was twice that of England. Ishbel launched a 'crusade' against the disease, largely focused on education and improvements in diet. For the first time, the death rate dropped. On the back of this success, she became the first female honorary member of the British Medical Association. She also managed to extract £25,000[22] from the British government to build a sanatorium for TB sufferers in Dublin. This money was not enough to cover children so she fundraised in New York among the wealthy Irish there and, when things got really desperate, she sold her own jewels.

Although Ishbel and John officially retired from public life in 1920, it was hard to get Ishbel to slow down. She continued working with the ICW, trying to rebuild an international organisation when delegates from countries that had been enemies during the war were so reluctant to work alongside each other. Thanks to her efforts, the League of Nations agreed that all of its roles would be open to women.

---

[22] Equivalent to almost £2.6 million nowadays.

She was greatly shaken by John's death in 1934 and the fact that – due to their debts – she had to leave their home, the House of Cromar, and move into Aberdeen. She became very interested in seances and spirit writing in an attempt to combat her loneliness. However, being Ishbel, this would not be conducted on a small scale. Her companion in all things spiritual was none other than Canada's then Prime Minister William Lyon Mackenzie King, who visited her in Aberdeen in 1937 on his way to a meeting with Hitler, whom Ishbel was far more sceptical about than the Prime Minister was. It was typical of Ishbel – mixing the domestic and personal with politics in order to move outside the sphere prescribed to women.

18. DR ROBERT HENDERSON

Britain's Iron Lung Pioneer (who Dated the Iron Lady)

1902 - 1999

Polio is a potentially lethal disease which can kill by paralysing the respiratory muscles; the patient suffocates to death. Tragically, in the early 20th century, it was most likely to be caught by children. There was – and is – no cure and preventative vaccines had not yet been invented.

In 1928, two professors at Harvard School of Public Health developed a negative pressure ventilator, more commonly known as an 'iron lung'. This could be used by people who were struggling to breathe due to a loss of muscle control. Although it was chiefly used to treat polio sufferers, it also helped poisoning victims. It worked by placing the person's chest inside an airtight cylindrical drum. The air pressure in the drum would then be raised and lowered, causing the lungs to expand and contract and air to flow in and out of the body. Within minutes the patient would be breathing easier and their condition dramatically improved. For most patients, it was a temporary measure, but some would remain reliant on an iron lung for the rest of their lives.

In the early 1930s, young Dr Robert Henderson made a trip to the United States and saw one of these iron lungs in operation. On his return, he made his own version at Aberdeen's City Hospital, where he was resident medical officer. He worked alongside the City Hospital's engineer on evenings and weekends to put together the device. Robert bought supplies from local firms to fashion his makeshift contraption, which used ship portholes for windows and was mounted onto the base of a children's cot to make it easier to move.

But just because it was unconventional, that does not mean Robert did not know what he was doing. It is possible that Robert's early background in mechanics may have helped him in this project. He was born a farmer's son in Clatt, Aberdeenshire and during the First World War, his father took him out of school and apprenticed him at a local garage. One of Robert's teachers at Huntly School suggested to his father that Robert should become a doctor and special tuition was arranged so he would be able to study at the University of Aberdeen.

Whether Robert's first job helped him or not, the iron lung worked. In 1934, a few weeks after it was completed, it was used to save the life of a 10-year-old boy from New Deer, Aberdeenshire, who was suffering from polio. It was the first time an iron lung had been used to treat someone in Britain and the national newspapers picked up on the story.

The local medical officer of health reprimanded Robert. It might seem bafflingly short-sighted now, but the man was upset by the nationwide publicity and by the fact that Robert had not gotten permission to use the facilities at City Hospital to make his lung. Bureaucracy, it seemed, was more important than saving children's lives. This telling-off had devastating consequences: Robert decided not to send his draft paper on the case for publication. It was eventually published some 63 years later in the Scottish Medical Journal in 1997 when Robert was 95 years old.

A year on from his reprimand, Robert moved down to London where he became a deputy medical superintendent and, in 1938, he joined a Medical Research Council committee on 'breathing machines'. Shortly afterwards, the industrialist Lord Nuffield offered to manufacture and supply iron lungs to any hospital in Britain or the British Empire that wanted one, without charging a penny. Finally, Henderson's creation went into widespread production.

Nuffield supplied 1,700 iron lungs across the Empire, including 75 to Scotland alone. These were widely used until the development of positive pressure ventilators in the 1950s which largely made iron lungs obsolete.

During the Second World War, Robert became medical superintendent of the Southern Hospital in Dartford, which admitted more patients than any other hospital in England during the Blitz. The Royal Navy used 500 beds at the hospital and many submariners were admitted with tuberculosis. In gratitude, the Navy made him a Surgeon Captain, one of only two in the history of the Volunteer Reserve. Perhaps most importantly for him, this meant he was allowed to wear the smart uniform of a captain. In 1947, he was given a CBE for services to medicine.

By this point in his career, it seems clear that Robert was revelling in the life of a bachelor doctor, enjoying dancing, parties and good Bloody Marys. He regularly went on free cruises as the ship's doctor – on one occasion taking 58 pairs of socks with him.

In 1949, he met Margaret Roberts, later to become Margaret Thatcher, Britain's first female Prime Minister. She was 23 years old – half his age – and near the start of her political career. For the next two years, the pair of them went on various dates, from parties to regular Sunday suppers at the Southern Hospital. From Margaret's letters to her sister during this period, it seems clear that she cared much more for Robert than Denis Thatcher who also occasionally took her on dates during this period. But in September 1951, she accepted Denis's marriage proposal. No one knows why she did not marry Robert; maybe it was the 24-year age difference, maybe it was because he never asked.

Robert rarely spoke about Margaret, even to his wife Josie, whom he married in 1960, although he did keep some presents and her photograph for the rest of his life. As for Mrs Thatcher, Robert might well have been her 'one that got away' but she seems to have still thought of him fondly.

Her experience, through him, of the introduction of the NHS helped form her opinions on that organisation. They remained on friendly enough terms that when she was contemplating her son Mark's circumcision, she decided to write to Robert for advice.

Their relationship remains a footnote in history. But perhaps it is worth speculating on this: would the world be a different place if Britain's Iron Lung pioneer had married the Iron Lady?

19. PROFESSOR R. V. JONES

Father of Scientific Intelligence

1911 - 1997

In 1940, during the Second World War, Britain experienced a few months of relative quiet between the evacuation of Dunkirk and the start of the Battle of Britain. Prime Minister Winston Churchill knew that the country could expect a heavy aerial assault but he felt reasonably assured that attacks would come only during the day or on moonlit nights, times when they had a good chance of fighting back.

Much to his horror, at a meeting in June, the young physicist R. V. Jones revealed that the Luftwaffe probably had a radar-beam system that allowed them to locate their targets no matter how cloudy the night. Unlike the Royal Air Force, which had focused their efforts on training navigators to fly by the stars; the Germans had developed a system where the pilot just had to follow a beam. When that crossed with another beam, this was where they had to release their bombs.

Dr Reginald Jones had worked on radar and aircraft detection since before the war. A brilliant young scientist, he had received a scholarship to the University of Oxford and completed a PhD by the time he was 23 years old. However, as international tensions continued to escalate in the lead-up to the Second World War, he decided to leave academia in the hope of serving his country through research. He had not yet turned 28 when war broke out but went on to shape scientific intelligence in a way that is still recognised today.

The Germans' radar system was codenamed 'Knickebein', meaning 'crooked leg' because the beams crossed each other. By following it, the bombers would be able to get within one square mile of their targets. The British codenamed this system 'Headaches'. Reginald, always something of a practical joker, came up with the cure for the headaches: 'Aspirins'. In essence, he developed a beam of his own which interfered with the Germans' system. It made enemy pilots go off the line that they were supposed to be following, meaning that they missed their targets.

His defensive ingenuity effectively started the Battle of the Beams. The Reich developed ever more sophisticated radar systems and the British, led by Reginald, came up with new ways of thwarting them.

Sometimes discoveries were made through luck, rather than scientific prowess. He received decoded messages from the Enigma team, referencing something called 'Wotan'. Reginald remembered how the codename 'Knickebein' referenced the way the beam worked and wondered if the codename itself could reveal the secret to stopping the Germans' new system. Knowing that Wotan was an ancient German god, he phoned up a friend at Bletchley Park and together they concluded that this reference to a one-eyed god must mean a radar system that used only one beam to navigate. Ironically, he discovered after the war was over that the system's codename was just a coincidence; there had never been any intention to link the name to the idea of one eye.

Nonetheless, because of this hunch, Reginald was able to figure out the Wotan system before the Germans even started using it. It was indeed a one-beam system and happened to operate on the same frequency as the BBC television transmitter at Alexandra Palace. Reginald's countermeasure involved sending a false signal from the television transmitter to make the systems 'ring' with feedback, almost like a microphone that gets too close to its loudspeakers. This false signal made it impossible to use. Thanks to Reginald's hunch, they managed to successfully target the Wotan system from the very first night it was used on a large scale. It was not long until the Luftwaffe gave it up entirely.

Although the German planes could hardly miss a target as large as London or many of the port cities, they were effectively lost when it came to bombing inland. Britain had won the Battle of the Beams and by the end of May 1941, the Blitz was largely over. Had it not been for Reginald and his deduction that the Luftwaffe were using a radar system, the Blitz would have been a far more lethal operation and could have critically hampered Britain's aircraft production. It is possible that in those circumstances, a successful Nazi invasion of Britain might have occurred.

This was not the last time that he would prove of great use to the war effort. As Adolf Hitler turned his attention to an attack on the Soviet Union, Britain decided that their best hope of fighting back was through an aerial bombardment of Germany. Reginald chose to focus his attention on German radar which would be used to guide attacks on British bombers. His most notable achievement in this area was probably the deployment of window or chaff. This was shredded tinfoil that could be dropped by planes and on radar screens would look like aircraft. On 24 July 1943, 743 bombers dropped 92 million strips of tinfoil, weighing 40 tons (36, 287 kg) in total. On the radar screens, it looked like 11,000 bomber planes were flying through German airspace.

This was just one instance where his trickster nature helped him come up with a cunning plan to deceive the enemy. He also came up with the idea of sending fake radio traffic to German submarine operators. This was to convince them that the Allies had detected their routes through infrared sensors, rather than the truth: that Bletchley Park had broken the Nazi codes.

After the war was over, Reginald was frustrated by having to operate in a committee. It was a real restraint on a man who had been in charge of scientific intelligence throughout the war. He decided to leave. A colleague from the Air Ministry had returned to his job at the University of Aberdeen and suggested that Reginald apply for a position in the physics department. Reginald was sceptical that he would get the job, particularly as his work in intelligence meant that he had not been able to publish any significant academic papers for the last 10 years. Fortunately, he had one formidable ally. A week before the interview, Churchill had visited the university to receive an honorary degree. Every time he bumped into the Principal that day, the former Prime Minister insisted that he must give Reginald the job. Unsurprisingly, he got the position.

Reginald remained at the University of Aberdeen for the next 35 years and the rest of his career. He briefly returned to intelligence work when Churchill was re-elected but again was unable to tolerate the peacetime restrictions. It took a long time for him to receive the recognition he deserved but towards the end of his life, he was lavished with honours. The CIA created the R. V. Jones Intelligence Award in his honour, which is given to members of intelligence services who demonstrate 'Scientific Acumen Applied With Art in the Cause of Freedom.' A year later, the Queen made him a Companion of Honour; an order restricted to a maximum of 65 living people at one time.

But perhaps the greatest accolade came from Churchill, who summed up Reginald's wartime work and his subsequent lack of recognition: 'He did more to save us from disaster than many who are glittering with trinkets.'

20. DR ROBERT 'ROBIN' DANIEL LAWRENCE

Champion of Diabetics

1892 - 1968

In the first half of the 20th century, there was an extraordinary amount of prejudice towards people with diabetes. Employers would see them as a liability, fearing they could fall into a coma at any moment; by disclosing their condition, some diabetics lost their jobs. In the 1950s, people diagnosed with diabetes were not allowed to emigrate to Australia. Before the formation of the National Health Service, diabetics found it difficult to get health insurance and it was not until after the Second World War that car insurers would cover them. Essentially, diabetes was still viewed by many as a death sentence or, at the very least, one which would severely impair the sufferer's quality of life.

The man who did more to change attitudes towards diabetes than anyone else was Dr Robert Lawrence. He not only set up support systems for diabetics but he also conducted a vast amount of research. As a doctor, he made the diagnosis a lot less scary and taught his patients how they could have a normal life despite their condition.

He knew what it was they were going through. After all, he had been on the receiving end of that diagnosis himself.

Robin was born in Aberdeen to comfortably middle-class parents. His father was a brush-maker who supplied Queen Victoria and the rest of the Royal family at Balmoral Castle in Deeside. Excelling both in the classroom and on the sports field, Robin even took a prize for 'sword feats on a bicycle' while at Aberdeen Grammar School. He started studying medicine at the University of Aberdeen in 1910. It was his dream to become a surgeon and he was such an accomplished student that after he had qualified, he was taken on as an assistant surgeon in the ear, nose and throat department at King's College Hospital in London.

But a freak accident in November 1920 was to prove a turning point. While he was practising an operation on a corpse, a chip of bone flew off and went into his left eye, which soon turned septic. There were fears he might lose the sight in that eye but that concern was put on the backburner when a routine urine test revealed high sugar levels. Biochemist George Harrison found Robin's blood sugar levels were three times the normal amount. A diagnosis soon followed: Robin was a type 1 diabetic.

Diabetes is when your body is unable to regulate your sugar levels in your blood. Non-diabetics control their sugar levels through insulin, which is produced by the pancreas. Type 1 diabetics are not able to produce insulin, meaning their blood sugar can reach dangerously high levels. This leaves them vulnerable to other diseases but also means they will begin to suffer neuritis (numbness in their hands and feet) and eventually slip into a coma before dying.

Nowadays, diabetics can regulate their blood sugar levels with insulin but that was not an option in 1920 as insulin was not available. The only 'cure' for diabetes was a brutally restricted diet which might extend life by a couple of years. Some diabetics who followed this system died not from their disease but by starving to death.

It seems that the most immediate impact of this on Robin's life was not his death-sentence diagnosis, but that he would always have limited vision in his left eye, destroying his dreams of becoming a surgeon. He moved to the biochemistry lab at King's. Under the supervision of Dr Harrison, the same doctor who had diagnosed him, Robin started work on his thesis about how sugar levels could be used to diagnose a patient with diabetes.

For both Robin and those researching diabetes[23], 1922 was a significant year. In January, the first experiments with insulin on a human patient were conducted. Although the results were promising, it would be a while before insulin was available to all diabetics. Meanwhile, Robin was starting to feel the effect of his diabetes and noticed that hard work at the hospital made it much worse. At 29 years old, he knew his days were numbered. He only had one decision to make: how was he going to spend them?

He decided not to go home to Aberdeen. He did not want to put his mother and father through the months of inevitable, irreversible slow decline, finally seeing him fall into a coma and die. Instead, Robin moved to Florence and worked as a GP, catering to the needs of the city's English-speaking population. He enjoyed the dancing, tennis and art, but when he contracted bronchitis, his health took a severe turn for the worse. Robin gradually got sicker and sicker, regularly falling, unable to walk upstairs and even falling asleep while talking to patients. When he developed peripheral neuritis, he started to question whether an existence where he could not even light a cigarette was really worth living.

Finally, in April 1923, insulin became available for patients in the UK who were no longer able to control their diabetes through diet. Dr Harrison sent a telegram to his friend and former colleague: 'I've got insulin come back quickly it works.'

One month later, with probably only weeks to live, Robin set off for London. He drove back with an Italian who wanted to visit his son in England. This man did not want to drive on the left in Britain so for the last stage of the 10-day journey, Robin had to take over. With severely limited vision in his left eye and in a state of near exhaustion, Robin made it through London and arrived at King's College Hospital on 28 May.

---

[23] See Bonus Bio below on J.J.R Macleod.

He was immediately taken in as a patient but he and Dr Harrison decided to delay the insulin injections. It was such a new drug that they wanted to be able to work out its clinical effectiveness by doing tests before and after. Three days later, Robin received his first dose. Neither of them had any idea how much to give since Dr Harrison had only treated three patients with insulin at that time. They settled on 20 units as it was 'a nice round figure'.

Insulin saved Robin's life. Over the next two months, he remained an in-patient at the hospital, but his health rapidly improved, to the extent that he was allowed out of the hospital, once being let in at 4am after he had gone out dancing.

After this, Robin dedicated the rest of his life to the treatment of diabetes, eventually becoming head of the diabetic department at King's. The way that UK diabetics are treated to this day remains influenced by him. He was an early advocate of teaching patients to inject their own insulin, something which helped them to manage their diabetes without constant medical involvement. He also made diet a cornerstone of his treatment plan and developed simple systems that allowed diabetics to work out what and how much they should be eating. As he often said to his colleagues, patients eat food, not calories. His book *The Diabetic Life* explored this further, giving advice on how to live a normal life with diabetes. This book ran to 17 editions and was translated into numerous other languages.

His fundamental belief was that patients should be enabled to manage their own healthcare. He took the time to show them that their lives could go on as normal. As one child patient recalled, he considered diabetes no worse an affliction than having 'flat feet or red hair'. Robin took particular care of child diabetics and even after his stroke, he went to their Christmas party at King's, joining in the fun by using his walking stick to play hockey with an orange. In one of his obituaries, it was said of his relationship with his patients that he 'seemed to know them all by name and he appeared to be acquainted with the personal problems of most of them'.

Along with his patient, science fiction writer H.G. Wells, Robin set up the Diabetes Association in 1934. The idea behind it was to create a community of diabetics working together for the greater good of all and helping to cater to specific needs that particular sub-groups might have. Within the Diabetics Association, patients and medical experts worked together, rather than doctors having the ultimate authority. Soon they were setting up holiday camps for diabetic children, allowing them to meet others with the same condition and giving their parents a break. During the war, Robin and the charity campaigned successfully for diabetics to receive extra protein rations. The Association, now known as Diabetes UK, was a huge inspiration for diabetic charities in other countries and nowadays, it claims to be the largest voluntary organisation in the healthcare sector.

Robin also did a tremendous amount of research, publishing a whopping 106 research papers on diabetes, including on the diabetic coma and diabetes in pregnancy. He was helped by the fact that he could experiment on himself, but the doctor was far from the perfect patient. If Robin went out for dinner and wanted to eat something that would affect him badly, he would calculate the amount of insulin he needed to balance himself out and inject himself through his trousers.

Having lived 48 years as a diabetic, Robin died in 1968. Throughout his 45 years on insulin, he remained true to a belief described by one of his longest-standing patients, 'Never let diabetes stop you doing anything you want to. And remember you must control your diabetes: never let it control you.' Thanks to people like Dr Robin Lawrence, that belief had become a reality, as a previously fatal condition has now been rendered perfectly manageable.

Bonus Bio: Professor John James Rickard Macleod
1876 - 1935

A few decades before Robin Lawrence, another boy attended Aberdeen Grammar School before going on to study medicine at the University of Aberdeen. His name was John Macleod. He became a biochemistry researcher and lecturer before moving to the University of Toronto in 1918. It was in his research laboratory that Frederick Banting and Charles Best managed to extract insulin and prove that it could be used to treat diabetes. John was awarded the Nobel Prize in Medicine alongside Banting in 1923.

However, John's reputation suffered because Banting widely denied that John had contributed at all to their discovery. John did not defend himself against these accusations and in 1928 returned to work at the University of Aberdeen, dying in 1935. In the 1980s, the circumstances surrounding the discovery of insulin were re-examined and it is widely acknowledged that without John's advice, help and support, it would have taken far longer to extract insulin. If that had been the case, many more people would have died in the meantime, including Robin Lawrence.

21. ISABELLA MACDUFF, COUNTESS OF BUCHAN

Kingmaker in a Cage

Died after 1313

Sometimes hiding within a well-known historical story is a character whose unusual life inspires more questions than answers. Such is the case with Isabella MacDuff.

Isabella was the daughter of Duncan, Ninth Earl of Fife. Her husband was John Comyn, Earl of Buchan, who had exchanged his lands in Galloway for control over the North East of Scotland. He was also prominent in the movement to regain Scottish independence, fighting back under King John against King Edward I of England. It is thought that he may have even fought alongside William Wallace at the Battle of Falkirk. However, along with many other members of the Scottish nobility, he eventually submitted to King Edward's domination.

This might have been the end of the struggles for Scottish independence if it had not been for Robert the Bruce. He decided that he wanted to restore freedom to Scotland, only this time he, and not John Balliol, would be king. To that end, he arranged to meet the powerful Scottish noble, John the Red Comyn (Isabella's cousin by marriage), to discuss things further. Despite having shared the governorship of Scotland, Bruce and Comyn were old rivals – and Isabella was soon caught in the middle of their feud.

They met at Greyfriars Church in Dumfries, supposedly because there would be no violence committed in a religious building. But tensions soon resurfaced and Bruce stabbed Comyn. The story goes that Bruce ran out of the church to where his men were waiting for him and said: 'I think I have killed John the Red Comyn.' His kinsman told him not to worry, that he would go inside and 'make sure' that Comyn was dead.

Bruce now had a significant problem: it would be difficult to become King of Scots if he was excommunicated from the Church and this was very likely to happen once the Pope heard that he had killed someone in a holy building.

The decision was made to crown Bruce as quickly as possible so that he would be king before the Pope kicked him out of the Church. Six weeks after he killed Sir John, on 23 March 1306, Bruce was crowned King of Scots. And two days later, he was crowned King of Scots again.

Traditionally, the Earl of Fife would crown the King – but the Earl of Fife at the time was an 11-year-old living in England under the careful watch of King Edward. In his place was his sister Isabella MacDuff, Countess of Buchan, who arrived a day after Bruce's hasty inauguration. Because the presence of a MacDuff added legitimacy to proceedings, the coronation was performed once again and this time Isabella crowned Bruce.

Isabella never saw her husband again. It is unlikely that he would have been able to forgive her support for the man who had killed his cousin. In fact, Bruce followed up this murder by heading to Aberdeenshire and fighting the Battle of Inverurie against the Earl of Buchan in 1308. This was the preface to the 'Hardship of Buchan', as Bruce proceeded to burn significant parts of the North East of Scotland to the ground and slaughter anyone who supported the Earl, with the aim of wiping out any support for the Comyns in this part of the world. John Comyn fled to England, where he died later that same year.

Isabella suffered greatly for her support for Bruce. Her starring role at the coronation meant that she had thrown in her lot with Bruce, whose forces were almost immediately attacked by the English. Along with Bruce's wife and daughter, Isabella fled north, perhaps hoping to make it to Orkney where one of Bruce's sisters was queen. They were intercepted by Balliol loyalists and became prisoners of the English.

Isabella and Bruce's sister Marjorie were singled out for a particularly nasty punishment. Sent to Berwick Castle and Roxburgh Castle respectively, they were kept in cages, with only a small privy for privacy. Although there is some historical debate about whether the cages were completely open to the elements, King Edward I's instructions seem to admit little doubt: 'Let her be closely confined in an abode of stone and iron made in the shape of a cross, and let her be hung up out of doors in the open air at Berwick, that both in life and after her death, she may be a spectacle and eternal reproach to travelers.' It was a punishment intended to humiliate and break the spirit. Isabella was kept in these conditions for the next four years.

Eventually, she was moved to the Carmelite Friary and later became a prisoner of her husband's nephew by marriage, Sir Henry de Beaumont. After this point, she disappears from the record so we can only speculate as to what happened to her.

Indeed, speculate is all we can do about most of Isabella's life. What motivated her to support Bruce? Was she a Scottish patriot? Or was this a personal matter? Perhaps she had a terrible marriage and this was her way of revenging herself on her husband. We shall never know for certain, for Isabella remains a mysterious figure in the well-known story of Robert the Bruce.

22. DR ALEXANDER MACKLIN

Member of Shackleton's Unlucky Expedition to Antarctica

1889 - 1967

Alexander Macklin was no ordinary doctor. By the time he was 27, his participation in Sir Ernest Shackleton's ill-fated Endurance Expedition meant he had travelled to Antarctica, had abandoned ship along with the rest of the crew and spent the next nine months exposed to the polar region's punishing climate, before eventually returning to civilisation. But whereas most people would consider that enough excitement for a lifetime, he sought out further life-endangering situations, such as serving in both World Wars or returning on Shackleton's next trip to Antarctica.

This perhaps makes it all the more remarkable that he eventually settled down – in Cults, Aberdeen. Hardly where you would imagine a thrill-seeking polar explorer ending up.

In 1914, the recently qualified Alexander joined Shackleton's Endurance Expedition. This was officially known as the Imperial Trans-Antarctic Expedition. The South Pole had been reached three years earlier in 1911. The aim of this expedition was to do one better: to be the first to cross Antarctica.

The Endurance Expedition never even made it to the continent. As they sailed towards their landing point on mainland Antarctica, their ship, the Endurance, became stuck in the frozen Weddell Sea and remained there throughout the Antarctic winter of 1915. Eventually, in October that year, the ship was crushed by the ice and sank. Before the Endurance disappeared below the water, the crew salvaged as much as they could, including three lifeboats. No one back home knew where they were or that they had lost their ship. If they were going to be rescued, they would have to do it themselves.

Despite these incredibly bleak circumstances, Alexander remained largely optimistic. He kept diaries throughout this period. The first night after the ship had gone down, he wrote: 'Really, this sort of life has its attractions. I read somewhere that all a man needs to be happy is a full stomach and warmth, and I begin to think it is nearly true.'

It seems that the hardest part for him was the death of his dogs. He had been given a team of dogs to drive and had formed a close attachment to them. When the ship was abandoned, the dogs had to be shot. Alexander's team of dogs were the last to be killed. When the time came, he was almost physically sick. After all the dogs were shot, he had to prepare the meat for the men to eat. Still, that was an easier task than killing the first puppy – a dog called Sirius who had never taken to the dog sleigh harness. Every time he tried to push the dog away to shoot him, Sirius would jump up and try to lick Alexander's hand. When he eventually shot him, Alexander was shaking so badly that he had to shoot a second time to finish Sirius off.

With no ship, the crew were forced to spend months on the ice. Throughout the Antarctic summer, the ice melted, broke apart and began drifting northwards. In April 1916, the crew took to the lifeboats and reached Elephant Island, an uninhabited and inhospitable place. During their journey in the open boats, they were regularly soaked by seawater and temperatures dropped to minus-30 degrees Celsius. Once they were on the island, they were relatively safe but it was not a permanent solution.

They needed to get help. Shackleton decided that he and five others would sail one of the lifeboats 1,300km to South Georgia, a British Overseas Territory in the Atlantic Ocean. Because he was one of the doctors, Alexander was left behind to tend to the medical needs of the 21 other men camped on Elephant Island.

Many of the men had suffered injuries or illness during their time on the ice. Alexander and his fellow surgeon James McIlroy dealt with abscesses, infections, a heart attack, a nervous breakdown and a bad tooth.

One man had gotten frostbite in his left foot. It had become gangrenous and all the toes had to be removed if the infection was to be prevented from spreading. The doctors used the upturned boat in which the men were sleeping as their surgery. After six months spent in the same clothes, they were filthy. For the operation, the two men stripped down to their undershirts, the cleanest clothes that they had left. Alexander administered the last dose of chloroform to keep the man sedated while McIlroy chopped off the toes. When the man came to after the operation, he was given one of the last remaining cigarettes for being so brave.

Miraculously, Shackleton and his party made it to South Georgia. Unfortunately, because the Antarctic winter descended shortly after they arrived on the island, it would be three months before the crew on Elephant Island were rescued. During that time, they waited, gradually losing hope that anyone was going to return for them. Even the ever-optimistic Alexander was beginning to believe that Shackleton and the rest had been lost at sea. Then, on the morning of 30 August 1916, a ship was sighted. Alexander raced up the island to their rudimentary flagpole and hoisted up his Burberry jacket as a makeshift flag to signal to the ship. Everyone was hastily brought on board the rescue vessel and in the rush, Alexander left behind his jacket. As he looked back at Elephant Island, their home for three months, he could see it waving in the wind.

Like most of the men on the expedition, Alexander joined up to serve in the First World War after their rescue. He joined the Royal Army Medical Corps and was awarded the Military Cross. During this time, he wrote to Shackleton saying how tanks were 'tame' after Antarctica. After the war was over, Alexander and several others from the Endurance

Expedition decided to join Shackleton on his next voyage, known as the Quest Expedition.

Frank Wild, who wrote a book on the Quest Expedition, described how some of the men had been waiting two years to be involved, refusing to commit to a steady job so they could join the expedition when needed. He attempted to explain why they were so keen to go back to a place from which they had barely escaped with their lives: '...for such is the extraordinary attraction of polar exploration to those who have once engaged in it, that they will give up much, often all they have, to pit themselves once more against the ice and gamble with their lives in this greatest of all games of chance. Yet if you were to ask what is the attraction or where the fascination of it lies, probably not one could give you an answer.' This perhaps explains, as best as anything can, Alexander's constant quest for adventure.

On 4 January 1922, the expedition made it to South Georgia. That night Shackleton suffered a fatal heart attack. Alexander was with him when he died and had the heavy task of embalming the body of his friend and late commander.

This was Alexander's last trip to Antarctica. He did not entirely give up a life of danger, also serving in the Second World War. When war broke out, he returned to the Medical Corps as a major. He served in East Africa and when he retired from the army, he was made an honorary colonel. In 1948, at the age of 59, he settled down at last, leaving the army and getting married. He and his wife Jean had two sons.

He was a major resource for Alfred Lansing's book *Endurance*, one of the first accounts of the expedition not written by a crew member. Alexander was given particular thanks in Lansing's book for answering numerous questions, as well as supplying the author with lots of primary sources. Lansing wrote that he owed Alexander 'a debt that is difficult to express'.

Alexander spent the last years of his career in Aberdeen where he was in charge of student health at the University of Aberdeen and a lecturer in social medicine. But he always remembered his time as a polar explorer – and whenever his sons complained about the cold in the North East of Scotland, he would tell them: 'You don't know what cold is!'

Bonus Bio: Robert Clark
1882 - 1950

Alexander Macklin was not the only member of Shackleton's Endurance crew to have an Aberdeen connection. The biologist, Robert Clark, hailed from Aberdeen. Later in life, he became director of the Fisheries Research Station in Torry.

23. RACHEL WORKMAN MACROBERT, LADY MACROBERT

A Mother Remembered for her Vengeful Gift

1884 - 1954

In July 1941, a month after her youngest son had gone missing while serving in the Royal Air Force (RAF), Lady MacRobert donated a bomber plane called 'MacRobert's Reply' to the war effort. It was her 'immediate reply' to the news that her two youngest sons had died fighting in the war, leaving her childless and alone.

It may seem an unusual response to the deaths of one's children; but then, Lady MacRobert was an unconventional woman. She was born in New England, America, to very wealthy parents and saw little of them while growing up, as they preferred to use their combined fortune to travel the world and break mountaineering records. Her mother was Fanny Bullock Workman, one of the earliest professional female mountaineers. At the age of 47, Fanny achieved the record for the highest elevation climbed by a woman, after having climbed 23,263 feet to the top of Pinnacle Peak in the Himalayas in 1906. This record would remain unbroken until 1934.

Rachel's own interest was geology. She received a second-class honours degree from London University and then studied a Masters at Imperial College London, where she published papers on petrology in Scotland and the effect of glaciers on the Swedish landscape. She was among the first women to be made a fellow of the Geological Society of London, although, as she noted in a letter to her husband, the admission of women to this hallowed organisation probably owed more to the fact that the society was in need of money which could be provided by female memberships, rather than a sudden appreciation of the worth of women.

She met Alexander 'Mac' MacRobert when she was returning from a trip to India with her parents. The self-made millionaire had made his fortune through woollen mills in Cawnpore (now Kanpur) in Northern India. Such was his influence in the city, he was described as the King of Cawnpore. Not bad for a boy who had started work sweeping in the Aberdeen mills at the age of 12. Or for a man who boasted that he was so frugal he had worn the same toupee for 37 years.

Mac had already been married and was more than 30 years older than Rachel. Their courtship was not without conflict, chiefly over Rachel's views on women's rights. She was active in the suffragette movement in York and later justified the violence of the suffragette struggle by saying, 'Girls have no sort of life under present social conditions and the wickedness of men at large.' During their engagement, Mac found out that he was to receive a knighthood from the King. His fiancée refused to go to the ceremony with him at Buckingham Palace, saying, 'I will bow to no man.'

Once married, the couple spent a lot of time apart since Mac had to manage his business interests in India, a country Rachel disliked. Instead, she remained at Douneside, the MacRobert family home near Tarland, and raised their three sons: Alasdair, Roderic and Iain. She wanted her children to become independent and so by the age of two, they were encouraged to spend at least an hour outside by themselves. We know this thanks to *The Journals of Alasdair Workman MacRobert*. From his birth until he was a toddler, the staff looking after him were instructed to write this 'journal' about Alasdair's daily life as though it was written from his point of view. Their desire to ingratiate themselves with Rachel can be seen in the fact that she is always described in the journal as 'Mother dearest'.

In 1922, two significant events occurred in the MacRobert family: Mac was granted a hereditary baronetcy – and died, aged 68, from a heart attack. He left behind a fortune worth £264,552 1s 3d[24] and 10-year-old Alasdair became Sir Alasdair MacRobert of Cawnpore and Cromar[25].

Although Alasdair could have taken over his father's business, his own passion was for flying. In 1937, aged 25, he started his own business – the Indian Aviation Development Company, which would fly its clients anywhere in the world they wanted to go. On 1 June 1938, he flew to Luton Airport to inspect some planes he was hoping to buy to expand his business. As he landed, he seemed to lose control and the plane nosedived into a field next to the runway. Alasdair and his two passengers were killed.

His two younger brothers shared his passion for planes. In 1938, Roderic joined the RAF as a pilot officer. In the lead-up to the Second World War, he was posted to the Middle East. There was little fighting for Roderic until the Iraqi Revolt in May 1941, when a nationalist movement sought to expel the British with the support of Germany. On 22 May 1941, Roderic led an attack on a German airbase in Mosul, destroying Junkers and Messerschmitts on the ground – but he did not return from the attack. It is thought that on his way back to base, he may have been shot down.

On 30 June, just a few weeks after Iain had returned to duty from comforting his grieving mother, he joined a search-and-rescue mission for a bomber that had ditched into the North Sea, off Flamborough Head on the Yorkshire coast. He never returned.

Rachel was left with no sons, no husband and no parents.

---

[24] Equivalent to around £6 million nowadays.
[25] The House of Cromar originally belonged to Lord and Lady Aberdeen but Mac agreed to pay their debts in exchange for the estate after their deaths. See 17. Ishbel Hamilton-Gordon, Lady Aberdeen.

Iain's last visit to see his mother coincided with 'Spitfire Week', a fundraising campaign to supply the RAF with more planes. Iain had suggested to his mother that she could fund a bomber. On 31 July – just 32 days after Iain had gone missing – she sent a cheque for £25,000[26] to the Secretary of State for Air.

She wished 'to make a mother's immediate reply' by 'attacking, striking sharply, straight to the mark' in the same way that her sons would have done. She asked for the money to be used to fund a bomber which would be called 'MacRobert's Reply' and carry the MacRobert Badge. She added: 'I have no more sons to wear the Badge, or carry it in the fight. If I had ten sons, I know they would have followed that line of duty.'

The money was used to buy a Stirling bomber which came into operation in October 1941 and was involved in 12 sorties, including an attack on two enemy warships in Brest harbour. It crashed in January 1942 and the panels with the name were transferred to another plane which was shot down in Denmark later that same year. In 1982, the RAF dedicated a new MacRobert's Reply: a Buccaneer XT287. Nowadays, every aircraft with XV Squadron that is coded F is called MacRobert's Reply.

This was not Rachel's last gift to the RAF. In 1942, she donated £20,000[27] to supply four Hurricane fighters. Her generosity to the war effort and her tragic story made her a household name and she regularly appeared at rallies encouraging others to do their bit.

Rachel's legacy lives on through the MacRobert Trust, founded to continue supporting charitable causes connected to the family's interests. Though her sons had died, she was determined that they would live on through the many memorial bequests in their honour, from town halls and university buildings to academic awards across the

---

[26] The equivalent to around £700,000 nowadays.
[27] The equivalent of £500,000 nowadays.

country. Ironically, the MacRobert name probably has more visibility across the UK, and particularly in the North East of Scotland, than if all her sons had survived to a ripe old age. And that is all due to Lady MacRobert and her initial, unusual gift of a killing machine.

24. SIR PATRICK MANSON

Father of Tropical Medicine

1844 - 1922

As fans of *Jurassic Park* know, mosquitoes have been around since the days of the dinosaurs. The malaria parasite that they carry has been discovered in amber dating back at least 15 million years. But despite this, it took until the 1890s for the link between mosquitoes and malaria to be identified. This connection was made thanks to Patrick Manson.

Patrick is known nowadays as the 'father of tropical medicine'. Born in Old Meldrum, he studied medicine at the University of Aberdeen, before leaving Scotland for the furthest reaches of the globe, working first in Taiwan and then in Amoy[28], China. His first discovery was how the disease filariasis was spread. The filaria worm had already been discovered in human blood. Patrick started to examine the blood of his patients suffering from this disease and was intrigued to note that the filariae could only be discovered at night. He hypothesised that an insect must be responsible for spreading the filaria because the worm moved on to another stage in its life cycle when subjected to cold conditions – suggesting a connection to a cold-blooded creature – and because of the spread of patients.

He settled on the mosquito as the most likely agent, partly because of where it was found in the world and partly because of its night-time feeding habits, which tallied with the appearance of the filaria. Patrick set out to prove that this worm was spread through the bite of the mosquito.

---

[28] Now Xiamen.

His gardener, Hin Lo, already had filariasis. Patrick built a mosquito house for Hin Lo with a bench for him to sleep on. At night, a light was placed beside him and the door was left open for half an hour. The mosquitoes, who were attracted by the light, came to feed on Hin Lo's blood and were unable to escape once the door was shut. The next day, the blood-gorged mosquitoes were caught and could then be dissected. It does not seem to have been recorded how Hin Lo felt about being fed on by mosquitoes night after night in these experiments.

Through dissecting these insects, Patrick was at last able to show that filaria was present inside the mosquito. This discovery was all the more impressive considering that virtually nothing was known about mosquitoes and their lifecycle at the time. In fact, when Patrick wrote to the British Museum requesting any information that they might have on mosquitoes, they replied saying that no book on mosquitoes existed so they were sending him one about cockroaches instead.

At this point, filaria was his obsession, so much so that when his first daughter was born, he wanted to call her Filaria. But during his 23 years in South East Asia, he made many other discoveries, such as sparganosis, which was caused by tapeworms, and new forms of ringworm. In addition, he correctly hypothesised that schistosomiasis was spread by a type of freshwater snail. He also helped to establish the Hong Kong College of Medicine for Chinese, the first teaching institution in Hong Kong to fully accept Western medicine.

Having made his fortune, Patrick returned to Britain to retire at the age of 46. But the fall in the Chinese currency meant that his investments depreciated and he had to return to work. This unlucky blow for him turned out to be a blessing to medical advancement.

Patrick set up a private practice in London. He continued his research by examining patients who had arrived from tropical countries with unusual illnesses.

Remembering how poor his own education in tropical medicine had been, he began giving annual lectures to the students at St George's Hospital in London. It was not long before doctors on leave from the colonies started attending these lectures as well. Out of this grew the London School of Tropical Medicine.[29]

Partly through his teaching and partly because of his reputation, Patrick became a mentor to many younger doctors. One of these was Ronald Ross. Patrick had already written about his belief that mosquitoes also spread malaria. Unfortunately, in London, there was very little opportunity to prove his theory; he needed someone else to do it. Ronald was a surgeon-major in the army, based in India, and had written about his belief that malaria was not caused by a parasite but instead was an intestinal infection. While home on leave, Patrick met Ronald and convinced him otherwise, showing him the malaria parasite and explaining his mosquito-malaria theory. Through Patrick's connections, Ronald was sent back to India specifically to investigate malaria.

Over the course of the next three years, Patrick and Ronald exchanged almost 200 letters. Ronald grew frustrated at the difficulties of experimenting on humans and eventually followed Patrick's advice to work on bird malaria instead. At last, he was able to prove Patrick's hypothesis on the link between mosquitoes and malaria. Although the two later fell out and Ronald tried to minimise the importance of his advisor, he paid tribute to Patrick in his final report, saying, 'His brilliant induction so accurately indicated the true line of research that it has been my part merely to follow its direction.'

Despite Ronald's work, many people remained sceptical of the mosquito-malaria theory. Patrick was mocked as 'Mosquito Manson'. He decided to resort to extreme

---

[29] Nowadays the London School of Hygiene and Tropical Medicine.

measures to prove his theory. In Italy, Giovanni Grassi had managed to cause malaria in a human volunteer through the bite of a mosquito. Giovanni sent Patrick some mosquitoes which had bitten patients with malaria. These mosquitoes were then encouraged to bite Patrick's eldest son, also called Patrick, who was studying medicine. Fifteen days later, he developed malaria, proving conclusively that malaria had to spread by mosquitoes since there was no other way someone living in London could have contracted it.[30]

The mosquito-malaria theory, the foundation of the London School of Tropical Medicine and his many other discoveries, all contribute towards Patrick being known as the father of tropical medicine. But another curious story shows how he had an unintended impact on the political fate of China.

One of his pupils at the Hong Kong College of Medicine for Chinese was Sun Yat-sen, later the first provisional President of the Republic of China and often called the 'Father of the Nation'. But Sun might never have become president if he had not survived his exile. After a failed uprising, Sun fled the country and settled in London. While there he was kidnapped and held in the Chinese Embassy, with the plan being to smuggle Sun onto a ship in a barrel and throw him into the Thames to drown. Thanks to a sympathetic cleaning lady, Sun managed to get word to his former professor that he had been taken prisoner. Patrick went to the embassy but was unable to secure Sun's release, eventually spending the entire night outside in a hansom cab so he could be sure that Sun was not removed without his knowledge. The next morning, he went to the Foreign Office and, under their political pressure, Sun was released.

It is yet another example of Patrick affecting the course of history and this one demonstrates his fellow feeling with the Chinese. When working in China, he was one of the

---

[30] The younger Patrick survived malaria but died two years later in a shooting accident.

most successful Western doctors because he made an effort to adapt to a different culture, learning Mandarin and practising in the open as the Chinese doctors did. Although his use of human patients for experiments would struggle to get past a medical board of ethics nowadays, it was probably his ability to win people over for use in his research, as well as his experimental thinking and scientific expertise, that allowed him to take such great strides to advance the course of science.

Bonus Bio: Sir Alexander Ogston
1844 - 1929

The lives of Patrick Manson and Alexander Ogston mirror each other in many ways: both were born in Aberdeenshire in 1844, both went on to study medicine at the University of Aberdeen and both were knighted for their contributions to medicine. The pair were friends, meeting first in London, where Patrick had gone after he had graduated aged 20, which was too young to practise. They corresponded throughout their lives and Alexander represented the University of Aberdeen at Patrick's funeral, laying a thistle on his coffin.

But unlike Patrick, Alexander spent a great deal of his career in Aberdeen, becoming a surgeon and a lecturer at the university. He was greatly interested in the work of Joseph Lister, who promoted sterile surgery. Following his example, Alexander introduced the carbolic spray to Aberdeen, making surgery safer.

Alexander wanted to find out why this improved the patients' chances of survival. Joseph Lister believed that germs were spread through the air and that the spray worked because it reduced exposure to the air. Alexander thought there was more to it than that. Working out of a shed in his garden, he was able to discover the bacteria staphylococcus, which he named after the Greek word staphyle, which means 'bunch of grapes'.

He injected these bacteria and the already known streptococci into animals, causing tissue infection and blood poisoning. Because of this, he was able to argue that suppuration of wounds and subsequent death were caused by these bacteria and that sterile surgery was the best way to avoid this. The British medical establishment dismissed his discovery and he was forced to publish his research in German. His work was accepted on the continent and gradually made an impact on the rest of the world. Nowadays, staph infections remain a problem; the superbug MRSA is a type of staphylococcus.

25. JAMES MARR

Heroic Age Explorer who Accidentally Prevented Nuclear War

1902 - 1965

During the Second World War, the British wanted to exert their authority over Antarctica. Rather than merely sticking a few flags or signs in the ground, the leadership came up with a plan to make the various uninhabited islands near the polar continent their own.

Despite fighting on multiple fronts, Britain devised Operation Tabarin, the only Antarctic expedition made by any of the combatants during the Second World War. The idea came about due to fears that the Germans or Japanese might attempt to establish a base in Antarctica. By 1942, it was clear that there was no threat from the Axis powers in Antarctica – but that did not stop Britain from looking towards the south.

Argentina had long asserted rival claims over Antarctica and, in 1942, it started to take action, by sending a ship to various uninhabited islands, pinning up Argentinian flags and leaving messages laying claim to all land south of 60°S and between 25°W and 68°34'W. Britain responded by sending a ship to replace the flags and messages with their own – only for their South American adversaries to return. To combat this, Britain finally launched its wartime plan.

To plan this operation, the government relied on the knowledge of experienced Antarctic explorers. Thanks to these men, the expedition went beyond its original aim to send some soldiers 'to sit somewhere in the Antarctic to occupy the place'. They believed that this mission could lay the foundation for post-war scientific research, with the plan evolving to include a semi-permanent base for exploration.

The man chosen to lead this operation was James Marr. Born in Cushnie, he had spent most of his adult life in Antarctica or the Arctic. In many respects, he was a prime candidate to lead such an expedition.

His first experience of polar exploration came under that legendary figure of 'Heroic Age' exploration, Sir Ernest Shackleton. For the Quest expedition of 1921 and 1922, they needed a 'boy' for the ship.[31] A national competition was run through the Boy Scouts and James was one of two candidates chosen for the post. At that time, he was halfway through a degree in classics and zoology at the University of Aberdeen but took time out of his studies to join the expedition.

In the following years, he made trips to both ends of the earth, discovering new islands, making biological collections and researching whales. James combined polar experience with scientific standing, which was just what the Operation Tabarin planners were looking for. However, James did have significant gaps in experience: for example, he was far more familiar with expeditions based on water rather than on land, and he had never actually led an expedition before.

What's more, he had less than four months to find a suitable ship, recruit volunteers for the expedition and source supplies and equipment. This was a formidable task in its own right: once in Antarctica, there would be no way of replacing anything for months on end. As if that was not enough pressure, he was working to a tight deadline to ensure they reached the continent before the Antarctic winter, with the added challenge of obtaining equipment at a time when many suppliers were also fulfilling military contracts. Somehow, James managed to pull this off. The expedition set out in December 1943, with several scientific

---

[31] To read more about Shackleton's Quest expedition, see 22. Dr Alexander Macklin.

experts – including a geologist, a lichen expert and, of course, Marr himself as the zoologist.

The original plan had been to establish two bases: one on Deception Island and one at Hope Bay on the Trinity Peninsula, which was attached to mainland Antarctica. This second base was where Marr and most of his party were to be stationed. The expedition members and their equipment were to be ferried there by two ships. However, due to the hostile weather conditions, the captains insisted that a landing in Hope Bay would be impossible. Instead, the men disembarked at Port Lockroy on Wiencke Island. One unexpected positive from the perspective of the expedition was that this had clearly been one of the landing sites for the Argentinian ship which had deposited flags and messages. Therefore, it seemed likely that they might return and the British could make a further claim to the land by already occupying it.

On the other hand, being on an island limited their chances of conducting significant scientific or surveying work. A big part of scientific exploration in this period was establishing a base and then conducting long sledging expeditions from it. The men hoped that the sea might freeze over and allow them to reach the mainland but it never happened. They did conduct some surveying work around Wiencke Island but, as one surveying party member pointed out, better results could be obtained from aerial photography on one clear afternoon from than all the work they had conducted over 24 days.

All of this left James deeply frustrated. He had not been able to establish a base at Hope Bay and his failure to do so weighed on his mind. Over time, those disappointments ate away at him.

However, there was some good news on the horizon. Towards the end of 1944, they received word that James and some of the other men would be taken to the Falkland Islands to talk with the governor about establishing a new base at Hope Bay. The original promise of Operation

Tabarin might finally be fulfilled; at last, they thought they might be able to make serious sledging expeditions leading to major scientific discoveries.

Some two months later, he returned. The men were struck by the significant deterioration in his health. It had been coming on for some time but perhaps the separation of a few months enabled them to see it more clearly. The expedition doctor diagnosed him as suffering from depression, along with the mental and physical toll that entailed. Plans were made for him to return home as soon as possible.

After Tabarin, James never returned to Antarctica, although he did continue his oceanography work. He also published a 460-page book on Antarctic krill, which is to this day a foundational text on the species. If asked, it seems likely that James would have deemed that the biggest success of his career, dismissing Operation Tabarin because of Hope Bay.

However, historians believe that the work done by Operation Tabarin played a key role in establishing scientific exploration in the post-war world. James had started his career in the 'Heroic Age' of Antarctic exploration and oversaw its transition from a time of individual ventures to government-backed exploration. Having set the standard for science in Antarctica, Operation Tabarin first became the Falkland Islands Dependencies Survey and is now the British Antarctic Survey, which conducts all British scientific work in Antarctica.

Ironically, it was the base that James was so disdainful of that went on to have the biggest impact. In 1957, Port Lockroy was chosen for tests into 'whistlers' – a type of electromagnetic wave – because it was the only place in the Antarctic region with a 24-hour electricity supply. These whistlers are a consequence of the earth's magnetic core. Researching them allowed scientists to work out a way to communicate with nuclear submarines while they were deep underwater. In 1982, this gave NATO a 'second-strike' nuclear capability and, when Russia developed its own technology, it became clear that any nuclear attack in the Cold War would be an act of suicide, leading to mutually-assured destruction.

In essence, from James' base – originally envisioned, at least in part, to prevent Second World War powers from conducting potentially devastating attacks – came a discovery which helped bring an end to the threat of nuclear Armageddon during the Cold War.

26. DR HUGH MERCER

George Washington's Greatest General

1726 - 1777

If Hugh Mercer had not died in the American War of Independence, he might have gone on to become a more beloved general than George Washington himself.

Hugh was born near Rosehearty to respectable parents, with his father the local Church of Scotland minister. At the age of 15, he attended Marischal College to study medicine. After graduating, he started to train to become a surgeon. Had it not been for the volatile political situation in the 18th century, Hugh might have completed his studies and lived out his days peacefully as a surgeon in Aberdeenshire. But his life was changed forever by the Jacobite Rising in 1745. Hugh and his family were staunch supporters of James Stuart, 'the Old Pretender', who would have been King of Britain if his father had not been removed from the throne for being a Catholic. Hugh joined the Rising under James's son 'Bonnie Prince Charlie' as an assistant surgeon to the army. He was even at the Battle of Culloden where the British Army eventually defeated the Jacobites.

To be a Jacobite in Scotland after the Battle of Culloden was very dangerous. If caught, at best Hugh would have been left to fester in prison and at worse killed outright. He went on the run and took passage on a ship bound for Philadelphia. He never returned to Britain.

In Pennsylvania, Hugh got further still from the reach of the British Army by heading into the backcountry and working as a doctor, helping all the dispersed settlers there. This existence was once again interrupted by war – this time the French and Indian War, fought between Britain and

France to determine which country would control North America. This conflict caused widespread panic in the colonies and people began to flee their homes. When the Pennsylvania militia was mobilised, Hugh became a captain.

In 1756, he was involved in the attack on the Native American village of Kittanning. Hugh was part of a small unit that became separated from the rest of their battalion and was attacked by a group of Native Americans. Everyone was killed apart from Mercer, whose arm had been broken. After having to reset his own arm, the legend is that he trekked 100 miles to Fort Shirley, eating berries and a rattlesnake to survive. It took him two weeks and when he returned, he was lauded as a hero.

Hugh was promoted to the rank of colonel a year later and was placed in charge of one of Pennsylvania's three battalions. British general John Forbes had arrived with a mission to retake Fort Duquesne[32] from the French. To do this, he brought together the Virginian and Pennsylvanian militias. It was at this point that Hugh first met Washington, who was the colonel leading the Virginian battalion. Hugh's unit was responsible for securing the road to the fort, which was then taken by Washington's men.

Towards the end of the war, Hugh was decommissioned. Not having a home to return to, he decided to move to Fredericksburg, Virginia, which was coincidentally where Washington had grown up. Hugh set up a thriving medical practice, with Washington's mother, Mary, on his list of patients. He got married and had five children, as well as acquiring a great deal of property, including Washington's childhood home, Ferry Farm.

But once again, Hugh's life was interrupted by the outbreak of war – this time it was the American War of Independence. Former Jacobite Hugh immediately declared his support for independence from the control of Britain

---

[32] Now Pittsburgh.

and its Hanoverian royal family. He became a brigadier general in the Continental Army and played a crucial role.

The crossing of the Delaware River is often held up as a pivotal moment in the American War of Independence. After months of defeats, the Continental Army was dwindling in support and morale was at an all-time low as, under Washington's command, they had lost more and more territory, including New York City.

However, on 26 December 1776, they launched a surprise attack on the winter quarters of German mercenaries near Trenton, New Jersey. Believing that the enemy would be sleeping soundly after the merriment of Christmas Day, thousands of soldiers crossed the icy Delaware River during the night and attacked at 8am. The Battle of Trenton was a rousing success for the Continental Army: they captured almost 1,000 German mercenaries while only losing four men. It was seen as a great triumph of military tactics and leadership by Washington and inspired the troops to keep on fighting – and the man behind the plan was Hugh.

They launched another offensive masterminded by Hugh one week later, leading to the Battle of Princeton. Because of the American victory at Trenton, a British-German army arrived on 2 January 1777 to engage with the Americans, having left a detachment of 1,200 men at Princeton. On arriving, they saw their enemy was camped on the other side of the creek. They settled down for the night and determined to attack in the morning. But under cover of night, most of the American army slipped away, leaving their campfires burning so as not to arouse suspicion.

The next day saw heavy fighting on the road to Princeton. Hugh was in charge of the vanguard of 350 soldiers sent to destroy Stony Brook Bridge. On the way, they ran into British forces and the battle soon became a race to the strategic position at the top of a nearby hill. Musket fire was replaced by hand-to-hand combat. Hugh's men were at a significant disadvantage as they had no bayonets on the end of their muskets. He pressed on, urging his men forward, but he was surrounded by British soldiers who mistook him for Washington and told him to surrender. As he refused to do so, they bayoneted him. Despite his injuries, Hugh was reluctant to leave his men so they propped him up against an oak tree to watch the fighting. The Continental Army eventually took Princeton and this success, as well as the Battle of Trenton, convinced the French that they should back the Americans and secured Washington's image as a talented general.

Poor Hugh seemed like he might recover from his wounds but, unsurprisingly given the standard of medicine in those days, he died nine days later. His legacy has lived on though, both through various places named for him, such as Mercer County, New Jersey, and in the achievements of his descendants, which include legendary Second World War General George Patton and *Moon River* lyricist Johnny Mercer. He could never have predicted it but, then again, he could never have predicted any of the strange twists that his life took.

Bonus Bio: William Thornton
1759 - 1828

Another doctor who graduated from Marischal College was William Thornton. An amateur architect, he went on to create the winning design for the Capitol Building, home to the United States Congress, in Washington D.C.

27. LORNA MOON

Woman of Mystery and Hollywood Screenwriter

1886 - 1930

In 1920, 20-something divorcee Lorna Moon arrived in Hollywood. It had been an extraordinary journey. She had grown up in the North East of Scotland where her father was a laird. Until the age of nine, she spoke only Gaelic and when she eventually learned English, it was at a convent in France. Before moving to the States, she had enjoyed great success as an actress on the Scottish stage and had been widowed by the First World War.

The only problem? Hardly any of this information – including her name and age – was true. They were part of the ever-changing narrative that Lorna wove around herself. The truth was perhaps even more amazing.

Lorna was born in the small community of Strichen as Helen Nora Wilson Low. Far from being a laird, her father was illegitimate and worked as a plasterer and landlord of a temperance hotel. He was an atheist and a socialist, with his garden shed earning the nickname '10 Downing Street' thanks to the political discussions that went on within. His radical views were to influence Lorna for the rest of her life. As a young woman, she longed to escape the restrictive and tightly-policed world that was a small Scottish village at the turn of the 20th century and dreamed of writing for magazines or newspapers in Edinburgh or London.

In 1907, she got her chance to escape: William Hebditch, a 29-year-old commercial traveller, stayed at the hotel and fell for her. On Christmas Eve, they married and moved down to his native Yorkshire, where Lorna gave birth to their one son, Bill. Much to Lorna's horror, not long afterwards her new husband announced that he had bought 160 acres in Alberta, Canada and that they would be moving there.

Lorna stuck out the life of a farmer's wife for a while but in 1913, she left William for Walter Moon. Although they never married, she took his name to give the impression that they were husband and wife. An added benefit to this was that 'Moon' sounded very like 'Doone' and Lorna's childhood heroine was Lorna Doone, the protagonist in the novel of the same name, who gets carried off by bandits at a young age but still retains her aristocratic poise. Inspired by this, Helen Hebditch became Lorna Moon. Together, Walter and Lorna moved to Winnipeg, where Lorna threw herself into the town's social life, writing for the newspaper and performing in local plays. They had one child, Mary, but at six months old, she was sent to England to be raised by Walter's family.

Perhaps Lorna would have settled down with Walter and been content that her childhood dreams of writing for a newspaper had come true – but her entire life was changed by a trip to the cinema. In 1920, she went to see *Male and Female* by celebrated producer-director Cecil B. DeMille. It was based on the play *The Admirable Crichton*[33] by *Peter Pan* author J. M. Barrie. Lorna took exception to the way that the source material had been changed and sexed-up. She wrote a letter to Cecil in which she 'razzed him wickedly'. Perhaps he saw something in her writing that he liked; in any case, he wrote back and challenged her to do better. Lorna packed her bags and moved to Hollywood, becoming a screenwriter or scenario writer during the silent era. Although now 34, she presented herself as in her early 20s and, despite never having married Walter, she said they were divorced for respectability's sake.

---

[33] Incidentally, the original play was a satire on Lord and Lady Aberdeen and their friendly relationship with their servants. See 17. Ishbel Hamilton-Gordon, Lady Aberdeen.

She worked on *The Affairs of Anatol* (1921), which was her first and only picture for Cecil. The silent era was a golden period of female screenwriters, who made up half the staff of writing departments in the major studios. It was also a time in which screenwriters themselves were famous, with their names listed in adverts to promote their films and their whereabouts reported in the newspapers. Within a year of moving to Hollywood, Lorna was already a media staple.

During her 10 years in Hollywood, she worked on films which starred Gloria Swanson, Lionel Barrymore, Norma Shearer and Greta Garbo. Her greatest success was probably *Mr Wu* (1927), starring Lon Chaney. Later, the *Los Angeles Evening Herald* would describe Lorna as one of the three best scenario writers in Hollywood.

But these were all successes that were yet to come. A year into her Hollywood career, everything was brought to a screeching halt when Lorna discovered she was pregnant. She had been having an affair with Cecil's brother William, who was also a screenwriter and, more importantly, married. It was while she was pregnant that she discovered she had tuberculosis, probably contracted when she was a child. The doctor advised her to terminate her pregnancy, as it would lower her immune system and increase her risk of dying from the disease. Lorna decided not to have an abortion, determined that her child would live, even if she could not.

She moved into a sanatorium where she started writing fiction, drawing on her Scottish upbringing for inspiration. These short stories were eventually published in a collection called *Doorways of Drummorty*. Her unromantic portrayal of life in a small Scottish community has been compared to the work of Lewis Grassic Gibbon. Back in Strichen, the locals were displeased to recognise themselves in her writing and her books were not stocked by the village library until the 1990s.

When Lorna's child was born, he was immediately taken away from her to minimise the chances of him contracting tuberculosis. He was taken to a crèche for homeless babies and from there was adopted by Cecil – the boy's biological uncle – and his wife, who named him Richard. It was not until he was 34 years old, after the death of 'uncle' William, that Richard learned who his real parents were.

Weakened by the birth of her child, Lorna remained in the sanatorium for a further two years. When she was released, her doctor warned her not to go ahead with her planned nose job to remove a bump she had got from jumping down a staircase as a child when she believed she was able to fly. The anaesthetic gas would have a terrible impact on her damaged lungs. Lorna decided to go ahead with the operation anyway, writing to her sister, 'In any case, I'll make a bonny corp.'

She survived the operation and her ill health did nothing to slow her down. Between 1926 and 1930, she worked on six films for MGM, including an adaptation of *Anna Karenina* called *Love*. The studio decided that the original ending to Leo Tolstoy's novel was far too depressing so Lorna had to rewrite the end. By this point, she was being ravaged by tuberculosis once more and she had to dictate the ending from her sickbed.

Despite being forced to move into a sanatorium again, Lorna embarked on a novel, set in a small Scottish community, which would focus on a young woman's burgeoning sexuality. This was too racy for her editor who wrote back asking if it could be about something else. Lorna hotly retorted, 'It is revolting to me that in a civilised world a woman's virtue rests entirely upon her hymen.' However, she did change the novel for more conservative tastes.

Incredibly, she managed to finish the book, even though her tuberculosis was now causing haemorrhages, sometimes several in a day. When this happened, she would be prevented from writing as any movement could cause another haemorrhage.

Despite this, she did not want her novel, *Dark Star*, to be promoted on the basis of its dying author, nor did she want to capitalise on a nostalgic view of Scotland, as exemplified in the 'kailyard' school of writing. Despite her rigorous defence of Barrie's play to Cecil many years ago, she did not adopt his rose-tinted approach to rural communities, saying, 'I'd rather be buried than be Barried.' Accordingly, her publishers were banned from putting any thistles or tartan on the cover of her book.

By this point, she was struggling to pay her medical expenses, forced to rely on charity from Cecil. She attempted to sell the rights to her novel to MGM but a book involving suicide off a cliff was always going to be a tough sell to a studio that had rejected the end of *Anna Karenina*. At the pitch meeting, her friend and fellow screenwriter Frances Marion stepped in. Knowing that nobody else at the meeting would have read the novel, she loosely based her description on details from the book but presented it as a comedic story about the squabbling Min and Bill. This last-ditch attempt to raise money worked and Lorna was amused to hear how her friend got her $7,500[34] for the rights to her book by brazenly lying to the studio.

Min and Bill was a huge success, taking $2 million[35] at the box office, the same amount as Charlie Chaplin's film *The Great Dictator*. Almost 15 years later, it was still one of the 40 highest grossing films of all time. But Lorna did not live to see it. She died seven months before it opened, on 1 May 1930 from yet another haemorrhage. Her devoted paramour Everett Marcy took her ashes back to Scotland to be scattered on Mormond Hill near Strichen. Various newspapers reported her age wrongly as 30 or 31; Lorna, who was 44 when she died, would have been delighted by this.

Some literary critics say that if her life not been cut short at the peak of her artistic output, she would have gone on to be one of the leading figures in Scottish literature, on a par with Grassic Gibbon. As it is, despite her Hollywood

---

[34] Equivalent to $110,000 nowadays.

[35] Equivalent to $29 million nowadays.

fame and colourful life, this Moon has been eclipsed over the years.

28. JOHN 'GENTLE JOHNNY' RAMENSKY

Safe-blowing Criminal Turned War Hero

1905 - 1972

On the morning of 26 March 1934, Aberdeen police were alerted to a break-in at the head office of Ledingham's bakery on Mount Street. This crime was clearly the work of a professional safe-blower as it required skill far beyond the capability of any local criminal. However, the police did have one clue to go on as their Glasgow counterparts had recently been in touch to let them know that the notorious Johnny Ramensky might be headed for Aberdeen.

Johnny already had a reputation as a peterman or safe-breaker. Having opted not to join any of the Glasgow gangs, he was known for being non-violent and was given the nickname 'Gentle Johnny' by the press. He preferred to target businesses rather than homes because these would be covered by insurance so it was a 'victimless crime' – and after his targets received their insurance pay-out, he could go back and burgle them again. He was knowledgeable about the different types of 'gelly' or gelignite and would only use enough to blow the safe open. One former accomplice said that he was the sort of safe-blower who wanted to tidy the place up after he had done the job.

After the Ledingham's break-in had been discovered, Superintendent John Westland got in touch with the Perth police and asked them to search the early morning train from Aberdeen to see whether Johnny was on-board. He was – and not only that, he and his companion were discovered to have £500[36] on them, a vast amount of money in those days.

Westland was charmed by Johnny's sense of humour during their interview. Johnny admitted that he had raided the property but said that he intended to plead not guilty, adding that he did not think Westland was likely to 'blab' on him. His plan was soon thwarted when part of a 10-shilling note was found at the bakery – the other part was found in Johnny's possession. He changed his plea to guilty and was sentenced to five years at Peterhead Prison.

It was his first time in Scotland's notorious prison, intended as a destination for hardened criminals and one of the most secure in the country. Within months, Johnny became the first man to escape from the prison itself.[37] To this day, nobody knows how he did it. One suggestion is that he used his incredible upper-body strength to hang from a ledge by his hands for half an hour, swinging over the top when the coast was finally clear.

The police were out in force to find him. A bridge over the River Ythan near Ellon was blocked off by the police on either side but Johnny crossed by swinging from the girders underneath the bridge and then hid in the loft of a garage until it was dark. When they finally caught up with him, he was holding an iron bar but, true to his principles of non-violence, he came quietly. In total, Johnny had been outside Peterhead Prison for a mere 28 hours.

This was typical of his prison breaks. Although he holds the record for the number of escapes from Peterhead, escaping four more times over the course of his life[38], the time he was free could be counted in hours and days, rather than weeks and months. He got a thrill out of escaping in

---

[36] Equivalent to almost £35,000 nowadays.

[37] Although other prisoners had escaped before, their escapes had been from the quarry where the prisoners worked, rather than the prison itself.

[38] Three escapes were made in 1958 alone when he was in his 50s.

the same way that he got a kick out of placing large bets or committing crimes. It was never about escaping long-term.

On his return to prison that first time, he was shackled. Even though his feet were swollen from his time on the run, leather anklets were placed around his ankles, topped with steel rings. These were joined by a chain, which was also attached to his waist. To move around his cell, he had to shuffle. So that he could change his clothes, his trousers and pants were split along the seams.

Johnny's reputation was such that the newspapers reported on this act of cruelty by the authorities and the issue was debated in Parliament. A few days later, Johnny was freed from his shackles. Never since then has a prisoner in Britain been shackled.

However, the Ledingham's bakery incident was not the only crime Johnny committed in Aberdeen. In 1938, he burgled the Empress Laundry on Seaforth Road. After he was arrested, he wrote a letter to the prison governor, saying that there was an unexploded charge of gelignite inside the lock of the smaller safe: 'I want precautions taken so no one may be seriously injured if it did go off.'

At many times during his life, Johnny lived up to his 'gentle' nickname. He was the stereotype of a jailhouse lawyer, writing many letters to the governor about his own situation, but also on behalf of many of his fellow prisoners. On one occasion, upon hearing that a detective superintendent he knew had been taken into hospital, Johnny sent the man a get-well-soon message, joking that time spent chasing after Johnny had clearly taken too much out of him.

But Johnny was to get a chance to prove his good intentions on a far larger scale.

When the Second World War broke out, Johnny, like many other prisoners, was desperate to get out. It was a great time to make money as a criminal, aided by blackouts and the black market. But Johnny's aim was different: he wanted to serve his country and join the army. When his sentence was completed in 1942, he immediately went to visit his old friend at the Aberdeen police force, Superintendent Westland. As Johnny ate a breakfast of bacon and eggs at the chief's desk, he became aware of people coming into the office on the flimsiest of excuses; they clearly hoped to catch a glimpse of the notorious safe-blower. Johnny challenged Westland to invite everyone up to meet him properly.

After Johnny promised to abstain from crime while serving, Westland wrote a long letter to MI5 explaining Johnny's particular skills and how they could be of use to the war effort.

The reference must have done a lot of good, because shortly after joining the Royal Fusiliers, Johnny was transferred to the Commandos and sent for training. During this time, he was sent on a tour around Britain to teach other Commandos about controlled explosives. He was then sent to Italy, where he famously blew open the German Embassy's safe and maybe even a safe belonging to Hitler in Rome.

But the details of his most impressive mission are still kept secret. We do not know how he managed to break-in to Nazi military chief Hermann Goering's headquarters, somehow accessing a bunker with eight-feet-thick walls and guarded night and day by 13 men. All we know is that he managed to do so and returned with secret Nazi plans.

While serving as a Commando, he wrote to Westland saying what an exciting time he was having and sending him two cigarette boxes, one for himself and the other for the governor of Peterhead Prison. Near the end of the war, their paths crossed in Lübeck, Germany. Johnny's Commando unit had been disbanded and he was working as a translator for the army. The superintendent was proud of all Johnny had achieved and wanted to give him a chance to put his criminal days behind him: he offered him a job. Johnny turned it down. What Westland did not know at the time was that as soon as Johnny's unit had disbanded, the seemingly reformed criminal had slipped back into his old habits, carrying out burglaries when he was home on leave. In fact, when he first saw his old friend in Lübeck, Johnny thought that he was there to arrest him.

Johnny returned to safe-blowing after the war – but he certainly paid the price for it. By the age of 50, he had spent 30 years in prison, the equivalent of three life sentences.

He also remained a figure of some celebrity. In the 1960s, he went into a café while on holiday in Ayr and soon discovered a crowd of a hundred-strong gathered outside the window, hoping to catch a glimpse of him. The police were needed to disperse the crowd. 'It is the first time I have ever had the police helping me to escape from anything,' Johnny remarked.

Unsurprisingly, he died in prison. During his second-last job, he had made an almost fatal mistake, falling nearly 60 feet onto concrete, perhaps because his failing eyesight made him mistake a shadow for a pipe he could shimmy down. These injuries contributed to his death at 68 years old in 1972.

Some people consider Johnny's life to be a story of wasted potential. He was a man whose daring, athleticism, ingenuity and compassion could have been put to better use than a life of crime. His time as a Commando certainly points to that. But before one rushes to that conclusion, it is worth giving the last word to Johnny. In 1951, he wrote to a reporter: 'Each man has an ambition and I fulfilled mine years ago. I cherish my career as a safe-blower. In childhood days my feet were planted on the crooked path and took firm root. To each one of us is allotted a niche and I have found mine. Strangely enough I am happy. The die is cast and for me there is no turning back.'

29. JOHN REITH, 1ST BARON REITH

Founder of the BBC who Helped Make D-Day a Success

1889 - 1971

John Reith is best known for being the first director-general of the British Broadcasting Corporation (BBC). As such, he probably did more than anyone else to create a broadcaster that is to this day respected across the world. He was responsible for many things that became central to the BBC's identity, such as impartial news reporting, arms-length management by the government and the BBC's World Service. He believed that the broadcaster should 'educate, inform and entertain'. These were so central to his vision of the BBC that they are summed up in the word 'Reithian'.

He also believed strongly that the government should not interfere in the running of the BBC. During the 1926 General Strike, he used the BBC to put forward both points of view, although, the BBC was still accused of bias from both sides. This brought him into conflict with Winston Churchill, who believed that the BBC should be a mouthpiece for the government. John believed that Churchill never forgave him for this; this belief was perhaps justified when in 1942 Churchill sacked him during a Cabinet reshuffle when John was a member of the government.

Churchill remained on John's 'hate list' for the rest of his life. As the name suggests, this was a list of the people that John hated most in the world. When he first met his future son-in-law, John explained to him in detail the concept of the hate list – and added that his daughter's fiancé was now at the top of it, beating Anthony Eden and Lord

Mountbatten. His former neighbour explained the reason for his sudden hatred: 'Only the fourth person of the Trinity would be good enough for the daughter of a Reith.'

Standing at 6ft 6in and with a dramatic scar on his left cheek, John certainly was formidable. He had received this wound while serving during the First World War when he was a young man. An astonishing disregard for his own safety marked his time at the front. He would regularly get out of his trench to walk around obstacles and once he even went to the toilet in no-man's land. One day, this bravado led to its inevitable consequences. He had gone out with his major into no-man's land to inspect the damage done to their defences. He was an easy target for a sniper's bullet. The bone beneath his left eye was shattered and the wound was five by three inches wide. As he lay on the stretcher, he bewailed the blood gushing from his face: 'I'm very angry and I've spoilt a new tunic.'

When John applied to the BBC in 1922, he did not even know what broadcasting was. Rather than researching the role, his main preparation for the interview was praying. But he did research enough to find out who would be interviewing him. The director of the board was Sir William Noble, an Aberdonian. John had already posted his letter of application but, fortunately, he had posted it in his club post box. Before the mail was collected, he persuaded one of the staff to open the post box. He rewrote his application letter, playing up his Aberdonian ancestry. This seems to have been enough to get him the job.

One of John's first innovations was the publication of the radio schedule in the *Radio Times*. This was a huge money-maker for the BBC and they offered John a share of the profits in gratitude. This could have quadrupled his salary but he refused, saying: 'The trade had put me in office; expected me to look out for them; there was a moral responsibility to them. I would have thought it hardly proper to accept the money.'

He was also the one responsible for the BBC becoming a public corporation. The organisation only had a licence to operate until the end of 1926 and he was worried that without 'the brute force of monopoly', other broadcasters would spring up, forcing down standards through competition for viewers. He put forward the idea of a corporation overseen by a board of governors who would prioritise public interest over profits. Thus, the BBC retained its independence and John established a model that was adopted by the Labour government in its nationalisation programme after the Second World War.

On the request of Prime Minister Neville Chamberlain, John left the BBC in 1938 to head up the government-funded Imperial Airlines. He appears to have regretted this decision for the rest of his life; when he was almost 70 years old, he put out feelers to see if he could get his old job back. When Robert Foot started as the new director-general in 1942, he got a phone call on the first day: 'This is Reith speaking, you really are not up to the job and you should go at once.'

When John started as director of the BBC, the organisation was a radio broadcaster. During his 16 years there, television evolved. When he left, he was given a television set - he said he would never watch it. But perhaps he succumbed to the lure of the TV for he had very strong opinions on the BBC's programming after he left. He said broadcasting greyhound racing was 'degradation and prostitution', while he described *Juke Box Jury*, a music panel show which ran from 1959 to 1967, as 'evil'.

As well time as director-general and his brief stint with Imperial Airlines, he also managed to carve out a political career. When the Second World War broke out, John got a position in the Cabinet as Minister of Information and became an MP. He was later elevated to the House of Lords. John was born in Stonehaven on 20 July 1889, when his family were on holiday there from Glasgow. In tribute to his birthplace, upon joining Parliament's second chamber, he became Baron Reith of Stonehaven in the County of Kincardine.

His time in the Cabinet was short-lived and he was eventually dismissed in a reshuffle in 1942 under his old adversary Churchill. He subsequently wrote to a friend in the Royal Navy asking for a job: 'I've only one stipulation - to be kept busy. By busy I mean about three times as much work as you imagine anyone doing.' He ended up being responsible for organising equipment and ships to be ready for D-Day. He was given access to top-secret details about the invasion. The Navy had anticipated that only 80% of their ships would be ready for the day; thanks to John, almost 99% of their ships sailed.

John was full of contradictions. Although he achieved great things, he could also be petty and small-minded. He did not seek wealth but he did want glory and attention. When he represented the Queen at the General Assembly of the Church of Scotland in 1967, he officially took precedence over everyone else in Scotland, except the Queen and the Duke of Edinburgh. When the car arrived to take him and his wife to the Assembly, she started to get in before him and he pulled her back, saying, 'D'ye not yet realise, woman, that I'm the Queen's representative in this land?'

Incredibly hardworking, he never felt his talents were put to good use, saying: 'What I was capable of compared with what I've achieved is pitiable.' He was a strict Christian with conservative values; when he interviewed would-be employees, he asked if they believed in Jesus. Despite this, according to both his daughter Marista Leishman and his biographer Ian McIntyre, he probably had a homosexual relationship with a friend of his, Charlie Bowser. In later life, he also tormented his young secretaries with his obsessions.

His daughter Marista perhaps puts all of his contradictions best: 'There is no doubt that he was in many ways a great man – a man hung about with greatness but festooned with littlenesses.'

30. MARY SLESSOR

Missionary who Wasn't Too Fussed About Religion

1848 - 1915

In 1997, Mary Slessor became the first women to appear on a Scottish banknote – the Clydesdale Bank £10 note which was in circulation until recently. In her birth city of Aberdeen, there is both a statue and a plaque in her honour. Yet she is far more famous in Nigeria, where she worked as a missionary, than she is in her homeland of Scotland.

Nowadays we find the idea of Victorian religious missions quite troubling. We see them as forcing religion on races that they considered inferior, another tool used by the British Empire to oppress and to expand its dominance.

In defence of the missionaries who travelled to the Calabar area in Nigeria, they saw themselves as righting an imperial wrong. The ports at Old Calabar and Duke Town had seen slaves exported since the early 1700s. This practice had a destructive impact on the surrounding tribes: life was valued cheaply, human sacrifice was commonplace and there were a whole host of superstitions to make sense of the fragility of existence.

Those who ventured forth to the Nigerian coast were of a self-sacrificing disposition. The area was known as 'the white man's grave' thanks to malaria and yellow fever. Some men who went there took their coffins among their luggage.

Mary Slessor arrived in the Calabar area in Nigeria in 1876 at the age of 27. She stood out from the other female missionaries because she was not middle-class. From the age of 11, she had been helping to support her family by working in the jute mills in Dundee. To prepare herself for this new role, Mary had been required to improve her education and got permission to read while she worked at the looms – an impressive feat, given that she operated two of the large looms, a task only given to the most skilled workers.

Technically Mary was not even a missionary; she was a female agent. Female agents had less freedom than male missionaries. They had to work in pairs and one of their responsibilities was to host afternoon tea for the captains of European ships. Mary was soon frustrated by this and got permission for a solo posting in Old Town. Throughout her time in Nigeria, she pushed further and further into the bush. This was often unpleasant and unsanitary; arriving at new postings, she might have to sleep on lice-infested sacks until she had built her own house. Her next request was to go to Okoyong, where one of her predecessors had been held for ransom and another barely escaped with his life. The only people who accompanied her were the orphan children she had adopted.

Throughout her life, Mary butted heads with tribal leaders and missionary officials. She defied convention even in the way she dressed: Mary mainly went barefoot and wore old cotton dresses, even shedding those if they got in her way. She cut her red hair boyishly short. Towards the end of her life, she went to a party held in her honour wearing a dressing gown as it was the closest thing she had to formalwear.

She threw herself into everything with enthusiasm and a sense of humour, whether it was cementing floors or vaccinating everyone in the community for smallpox. She never tried to force her religion on other people and saw African beliefs as co-existing peacefully beside her Christian faith.

Mary stood up against injustice, whether defending those accused of witchcraft or a slave who was to be punished because one of the chief's wives had taken a shine to him. She was well aware of how fragile life was in the tribal communities.

Her best friend Ma Eme only escaped execution after the death of her husband thanks to a dead bird. After her husband died, all his wives were suspected of being responsible. Each of them had to bring a white bird with them to the trial. The direction it ran after it was beheaded determined her guilt or innocence. If it had run the wrong way, Ma Eme would have been buried alive.

Mary's most significant impact was in changing attitudes around twin babies. Twins were often killed during the first few days of their lives as it was believed that one was the offspring of a devil and, as you did not know which one, you would kill both babies to be sure. Slessor saved hundreds of babies and provided sanctuary for their mothers who were often cast out from their communities. She also adopted nine children.

Her irreverence for authority and her defence of women's rights caused her even to question the Bible. In her well-thumbed copy, there is a note beside the section where St Paul talks about how women should show obedience to their husbands. Mary wrote: 'Na! Na! Paul, laddie! This will n' do!'

Ultimately it was her compelling personality that enabled her to bring about change and won her many friends in the country she came to call home. This is shown by a story from years after her death. A minister gave a presentation on her life to the patients at the Mary Slessor Hospital in Itu. To illustrate his talk, the minister accompanied it with lantern slides. After the talk, one of the patients spoke to him and asked to have the sheet the slides had been projected onto. When asked why, the elderly man said that Mary's image had appeared on that sheet, adding: 'She was my friend and I like that face too well.'

31. ALEXANDER STEWART, 12ᵀᴴ EARL OF MAR

Bastard Pirate Turned Powerful Earl

c. 1380 - 1435

The life of Alexander Stewart shows how volatile politics were in Scotland in the early 15ᵗʰ century. King Robert III was unable to rule and a succession of regents governed the country. The King's brother, the Duke of Albany, eventually gained control of the kingdom, shortly after the heir to the throne had died in suspicious circumstances – while imprisoned by Albany. In 1406, King Robert III died. His 12-year-old son James became King James I, the next King of Scots, but, in an attempt to put him out of reach of Albany, James had been sent to France and en route was captured by the English. He remained a prisoner at the English court for the next 18 years. During these turbulent times, Scotland was a dangerous place. Power was unstable and ever-shifting. One minute, you could be a king in your own castle and the next, dead in a dungeon. In such conditions, certain people thrive. Alexander Stewart was one of them.

Alexander's father was Alexander Stewart, 1ˢᵗ Earl of Buchan, known as the Wolf of Badenoch. He was the illegitimate son of King Robert II and his mistress but had become legitimate after his parents' marriage. The Wolf had done his fair share of contributing to the instability of Scotland by marauding all over the Highlands. He was most notorious for burning down Elgin Cathedral, after he had been excommunicated for trying to divorce his wife, and for the legend which attributes his death to a night spent playing chess with the Devil.

Alexander was one of the Wolf's more than 40 illegitimate children and the son of the Wolf's long-term mistress Mairead inghean Eachann. Being born out of wedlock meant that it was harder – though not impossible – to inherit lands and titles. But Alexander was still politically well-connected; one of his uncles was the king, another was the regent and his great-great-grandfather had been Robert the Bruce, King of Scots.

As a young man, he led a wild band of Highland warriors. It is supposedly with the help of these men that he managed to become the Earl of Mar. He did so by marrying Isabel Douglas, Countess of Mar. She had become the Countess of Mar after the death of her brother when there were no male heirs left to succeed. When her husband was away from home, Alexander Stewart is supposed to have attacked him and kept him prisoner until he died. He then besieged Kildrummy Castle where Isabel lived, taking her prisoner. During this period, she agreed to sign over the earldom to him and his heirs. On 14 December 1404, Isabel and Alexander were married in front of her tenants outside the walls of Kildrummy Castle.

In one fell swoop, he had gone from being an illegitimate nobody to one of the most powerful men in Scotland.

Alexander got away with all of this because the regent of Scotland was the Duke of Albany, who just so happened to be Alexander's uncle. Initially, Albany was unhappy at this aggressive move by Alexander – not because of the kidnapping and coercion of Isabel but because if the earldom went to Alexander's heirs, it excluded the current heirs, who were supporters of Albany. A compromise was reached, where Alexander was granted the title for life. If Alexander and Isabel had any children, the earldom would pass to them; if not, it would go to Isabel's heirs. Isabel died four years later, without having produced any heirs for Alexander. He eventually managed to get this agreement overturned by having the Crown bestow the title afresh on him, to pass after his death to his illegitimate son Thomas.

But Alexander's triumph was not absolute as his son died before he did so the title reverted to the Crown on Alexander's death.

After he married Isabel and became the Earl of Mar, Alexander played an increasingly important part in national politics. He commanded a fleet that attempted to blockade Newcastle upon Tyne and Berwick and was involved in various negotiations with the English. He was Admiral of the North Sea and also became the main enforcer of law in the North of Scotland, largely because of his part in the Battle of Harlaw.

The battle was fought two miles north of Inverurie, against Donald, Lord of the Isles. Donald and Albany both wanted to take control of the Earldom of Ross. This escalated into Donald rallying his troops and marching through Ross, Inverness and onto Aberdeen to fight Alexander, Albany's main supporter in the north.

Alexander hastily assembled an army, made up of local lairds and knights, as well as burgesses of Aberdeen led by Provost Robert Davidson. Both sides sustained heavy losses on the first day, but when the Aberdeen army got up to fight on the second day, they found that Donald and his forces had slipped away in the night. The threat to Aberdeen was gone.

This may have been a bittersweet victory for Alexander. Among the dead was Davidson, with whom Alexander had worked to commit numerous acts of piracy against English, Dutch and Hanseatic ships. This led to the Hanseatic League imposing an embargo on Scottish trade that was not lifted until 1436, some 24 years later. Davidson is most notorious for having captured a ship belonging to the Mayor of London, Richard 'Dick' Whittington. He was also taken to court in Paris by members of the Hanseatic League but, as the French Government had already given him a passage of safe conduct, he could not be given any punishment. Aberdeen Burgh Council even sent a letter denying that their Provost could be involved in piracy and asking for compensation for Davidson.

Some historians have suggested that Alexander started his campaign of piracy against the Dutch for romantic revenge rather than money. When involved in military campaigns in the Low Countries, he married his second wife, Marie van Hoorn – who later turned out to already be married to someone else. Although the marriage was eventually annulled, it is thought that Alexander may have blamed his Dutch companions for not having warned him and have got his revenge by beginning to plunder Dutch ships.

It seems a strange explanation for embarking on piracy. But then again, Alexander was a peculiar, unpredictable individual – something which probably helped him greatly in the volatile political landscape of Scotland at this time and assisted him in his main objective: looking after his own interests.

This can be seen in his actions when James I finally returned to rule Scotland. The regency had passed to Albany's son and Alexander's cousin, Murdoch Duke of Albany. Alexander, who managed to keep his influential position after the return of King James I, sat on the jury which condemned the regent, his sons and father-in-law to death for treason.

Born with no real power or prestige, Alexander's ruthlessness, unpredictable nature and political manoeuvring saw him grow into one of the most influential people in Scotland. His story is a chilling example of all that can be achieved with sheer determination and unyielding self-interest.

32. MARY ANN SUTHERLAND AKA MRS GORDON BAILLIE

One Woman, Many Names and Too Many Lies to Count

1848 - unknown

Wealthy, well-travelled and part of the upper classes, philanthropist Mrs Gordon Baillie appeared to have it all. She was a regular in the newspapers and enjoyed her life to the utmost – a life spent adroitly deceiving the aristocracy time and time again.

Born into poverty in Peterhead in 1848, she was the illegitimate daughter of a hawker or servant. As a young woman, she moved to Dundee, using the name Mary Ann Bruce Sutherland. She became a teacher, known for her Christianity and missionary work – but even at this time in her life she was a woman of mystery. It is still unclear to this day how she managed to secure this job or fund her comfortable lifestyle, given her impoverished upbringing. She did, however, have a habit of borrowing items and not returning them, even keeping underclothing loaned by her cleaner.

As her creditors began to close in, she left Dundee and embarked upon a career of deception and trickery. She next resurfaced in Rome, where she lived in a villa outside the city, enjoying the comforts of servants and her own carriage. Her modus operandi was to ingratiate herself with the local aristocracy who would readily lend money to this genteel lady – then when people started to become suspicious, she would flee town, often adopting a new name and identity, and repeat the process all over again.

Throughout the course of her 'career', she had more than 40 aliases, many of them titled or in some way connected to the Scottish upper classes; one time she claimed to be the Countess of Moray but that she was not allowed to take her title due a genealogical error. Her escapades took her all over the globe and she is known to have operated in Italy, Paris, Edinburgh, Liverpool, London, New Zealand, Australia and the United States.

Because of her constantly changing persona, some details of her life are unclear – she lived with at least two men as husband and wife but whether she actually married either is uncertain. Even the number of her children is unknown: when she arrived in Melbourne, she seems to have suddenly acquired two little girls; later in life, she was supposed to have four or five children. It has also been suggested that when she ran out of money, she put her children in the workhouse. Once fortune favoured her again, she returned to claim her children – only to send all but the youngest back when she had to focus on the serious business of defrauding high society out of their money.

Despite being almost illiterate, she played the part of an elegant upper-class lady to perfection and deceived numerous shopkeepers, bankers and wealthy men with her smart clothes and nice manners. Although she had no money of her own, she managed to lease 75,000 acres in Victoria, Australia. She used her ill-gotten gains to fund an extravagant lifestyle; for example, while in Christchurch, New Zealand, she sat down to a Champagne lunch every day. One of her victims went bankrupt in the process of paying for her house and funding her lifestyle, which cost as much as £15,000.[39]

That is not to say she was always successful in her deceptions as she was frequently arrested and sent to prison. But time behind bars seemed to take no toll on her

---

[39] The equivalent of almost £2 million nowadays.

physically and as soon as she was released, she would return to her old ways.

In 1888 she suffered her biggest setback when, under the name Mrs Gordon Baillie, she was tried for fraud and sent to prison for five years. But despite being exposed in the national newspapers, she still popped up in unusual places, attempting to convince people that she was other than what she was. There are records of her operating in Pittsburgh in 1912, pretending to be the former wife of a captain in the British Army. When the 64-year-old Mary Ann was arrested, she first tried to use tears to elicit sympathy for this frail old woman. When it became clear that she was not deceiving anyone, she instantly ceased the waterworks and stopped using her walking stick.

What makes Mary Ann so compelling is the fact that we still do not know what motivated her. It may be that she was driven by greed alone. It may be that she enjoyed performing different parts; she certainly contemplated becoming an actor on more than one occasion.

The thing that complicates these selfish motives is that she often used her position to benefit others, such as by holding a picnic for local children or going prison visiting. Perhaps these philanthropic efforts were just window dressing to her performance of a wealthy and upper-class woman. Or perhaps they were something more.

One group which she seemed to advocate for with genuine passion were the Hebridean crofters. At this point, the crofters were batting to win land rights and security of tenure. She visited the female crofters who had been imprisoned in Calton Jail in Edinburgh and made several trips to Skye itself. The 75,000 acres she leased in Victoria was to be used by any Hebridean crofters who made their way to Australia after having been evicted in Scotland.

Mary Ann made her views about the treatment of the crofters clear: 'Although I belong to, and have been reared among, the aristocracy, my sympathies are not with them. I think they have been guilty in too many cases of great injustice.'

Perhaps it was just another line coming from a woman who had made a life out of treachery and deceit. Alternatively, perhaps she was on the way to believing that she truly was a member of the aristocracy. As one Edinburgh professor whom she conned out of a guinea said, 'I verily believe she would have deceived the devil himself.'

33. DAVID WELCH

The Gardener who Managed a Nation's Mourning

1933 - 2000

Aberdonians are incredibly proud of the fact that over the space of 19 years the city won 10 awards at a national horticulture competition called Britain in Bloom, scooping top prize seven times over a period of 11 years. In fact, the story goes that Aberdeen won so many times, the British Tourist Authority had to exclude the city from the running every three years, just to give other entrants a chance to win. This botanical success story is almost entirely down to the efforts of one man: David Welch.

At the age of 33, David became director of Aberdeen's parks in 1967. At first, this was something of a controversial appointment as he was an outsider; so much so that one local newspaper reported him taking over the role with the headline: 'Sassenach gets Top City Job'.

David was indeed a 'Sassenach' or English man. He hailed from Nottingham, becoming an apprentice gardener at 16 years old. For four years, he worked in Blackpool, where he planted half a million antirrhinums a year to 'vie with the illuminations'.

Vibrant swathes of flowers became something of a calling card of his work in Aberdeen. He described himself as 'an advocate of floral vulgarity and swaggering excesses of colour', a necessary quality in a city so defined by its grey granite. The numbers tell their own story. Thanks to him, 12 million daffodils were planted across Aberdeen. One observer said that it looked like he had 'tipped a plate of custard' over the city. If that was not enough, he also planted crocuses – 30 million of them.

These were not the only changes he introduced into Aberdeen's green spaces. He overhauled the Winter Gardens[40] in Duthie Park, making it one of Scotland's most-visited tourist attractions by 1989.

But he is perhaps best in Aberdeen remembered for his roses. He planted the flowers down the central reservation of Anderson Drive. At first, the council was reluctant to fund the planting of roses and argued that it would be much cheaper to have grass. David decided not to get into an aesthetic argument and instead told the council that grass would cost them much more because they would have to send a man to cut it twice a month; if they planted roses, they would only need a gardener to prune them once a year. He got his roses. When he arrived, there were 27,000 roses in public spaces; by the time he left, there were two million.

A man who combined green fingers with the ability to manage people was a great asset in the world of public parks. In 1992, David was headhunted to become chief executive of London's Royal Parks, with responsibility for – among others – Hyde Park, Regent Park, St James Park and Kensington Gardens. By this point, he loved the city that had initially been so reluctant to accept him. David had lived in Aberdeen for 25 years and it was home to his four children. He decided to accept the post but to remain based in Aberdeen, commuting down to London every week.

With control over 5,000 acres of parks, his methods in London were similar to those employed in Aberdeen: the aim was always to add colour and to encourage people to use these public spaces. He planted daffodils in the Mall and Green Park. He got rid of 'please keep off the grass' signs and replaced them with welcoming noticeboards. He repaired the Hyde Park Lido and pedestrianised the area in front of Buckingham Palace.

One of the biggest challenges of his career came after the death of Princess Diana. In the vast outpouring of

---

[40] Now the David Welch Winter Gardens.

public grief that followed, flowers were laid across London, particularly in front of Buckingham Palace and Kensington Palace. It is estimated that there was as many as 10,000 tons worth of bouquets, messages and toys. These flowers could not be left outside the palaces to rot indefinitely but the situation had to be handled carefully since emotions were already running high. Further ire would be heaped on the Royal Family if it appeared that the peoples' floral tributes were disregarded and discarded.

It was part of David's job to deal with the problem of the flowers. He decided that the flowers and tributes needed to be sorted through individually so that each could be dealt with appropriately. To do this, he needed a lot of manpower so he recruited volunteers, including girl guides, boy scouts and taxi drivers.

The volunteers sorted through all the flowers, teddies, soft toys, poems, cards and letters left outside the palaces. Written messages were filed away for the Spencer family. Toys were given to underprivileged children. Flowers still in good condition were taken by the taxi drivers to nursing homes and old people's homes. Rotting flowers were mulched and made into compost which was spread in Kensington Gardens; 'flowers to make new flowers', as David adroitly described it.

If that was not enough, he also had less than 48 hours to prepare London's open spaces for the vast number of mourners pouring into the city for the funeral. To prevent those paying their respects from being crushed, some of the fences were removed. Afterwards, many of them were not replaced, helping to achieve David's overall aim of making the parks more open and accessible. Finally, he initiated the creation of the Diana Princess of Wales' Memorial Playground in Kensington Gardens.

The royal family were very grateful to David for the diplomatic way he had handled the situation. Because of this and their shared love of gardening, he became friends with Prince Charles. Three years later, Charles visited David in hospital the day before he died of leukaemia at the age of 66.

Flowers are often seen as a symbol of transience and ephemerality. But the flowers of David Welch's time in Aberdeen have formed a lasting legacy, because of the millions of daffodils that bloom across the city, heralding to many winter-weary Aberdonians the beginning of spring.

34. PETER WILLIAMSON

'Indian Peter'

c. 1730 - 1799

On a map of Aberdeen from 1789, there is a building labelled: 'The old barn where kidnapped boys were kept'. It was well known that children used to be kidnapped and sent to the American colonies as indentured servants. Indentured servitude was a type of contract where workers were essentially slaves for a set number of years, after which they would receive their freedom. This sort of labour was common in the 18th century, even for children. Legally, their contracts had to be certified by a magistrate and have the permission of a parent – however, this point was regularly ignored in Aberdeen. Some of the highest people in Aberdeen's society were involved in this trade, including magistrates and merchants. They paid agents to kidnap suitable children. At the height of the kidnapping, between 1740 and 1746, 600 children were sold into slavery from Aberdeen. Some of them were as young as six years old.

The most famous of these kidnapped children was Peter Williamson. He was born near Aboyne but at the age of 10, he went to live with his aunt in Aberdeen. Three years later in 1743, he was playing down by the harbour when two men approached him. They must have decided that he looked like a strong boy for whom they would get a good price.

They lured him to the barn in The Green. A piper was employed to play outside, partly to provide entertainment for the trapped children but mainly to drown out any cries for help. The children were allowed out to exercise on the shore and on the links. They were watched over at all times by a man with a whip.

Peter's father was able to track his missing son down to the barn but was not able to talk to him. He went to the authorities and was able to get a warrant for Peter's release but by the time he returned, it was too late: Peter had been shipped to the colonies.

It took 11 weeks to cross the Atlantic. They had just reached the mouth of the River Delaware when the vessel was caught in a storm. The captain and crew abandoned the ship with the children onboard. The ship was wrecked and the crew returned to pick up any survivors after the storm had passed – one of whom was Peter.

In Philadelphia, he was sold for seven years to Hugh Wilson, who was from Perth and had himself been kidnapped and sold into slavery as a child. He raised Peter almost like his own son, paying for him to go to school and learn to read and write. Five years later Wilson died, leaving him a small amount of money, his best horse, saddle and his entire wardrobe.

For the next seven years, Peter travelled around the colonies in North America, picking up jobs here and there. At the age of 24, he settled down with a planter's daughter in Pennsylvania. They had their own house, barn and 30 acres of land. Incredibly, everything seemed to have worked out for Peter.

That was until war broke out between the British and French colonies. Both sides enlisted Native Americans as allies. On 2 October 1754, Peter was home alone while his wife visited relatives. Peter's house was attacked by a group that he described as Cherokees, although it would be more accurate to say they were Lenape. Peter was taken prisoner, the house was looted and he was made to carry the stolen goods for his captors.

While Peter was a prisoner, he saw the execution of others who had tried to escape the Lenape. In particular, he described two prisoners who were tortured with fire and hot irons before being gutted. A third was buried up to his neck in the ground and scalped. A small fire was lit close to the man's head so that his eyes 'gushed out of their sockets'.

After three months' imprisonment, Peter escaped and returned to his father-in-law's house – only to find that his wife had been dead for two months. Peter then enlisted with the Pennsylvanian volunteers but when he was a soldier, he was captured by the French, making this the third time he was a prisoner. Fortunately for him, he was involved in a prisoner exchange and sent back to Britain, landing in Plymouth. Because of an injury to his hand, he was discharged from the army and given six shillings.[41]

Peter made it as far as York before running out of money. There he persuaded a local businessman to fund the publication of his memoirs. It was perhaps the original misery memoir. It is worth saying that Peter's claims about his kidnapping and treatment by the Lenape have been questioned. He certainly knew that his time with the Lenape would be the book's main selling point. The cover had a picture of him wearing the outfit, headdress and war paint of a Native American. When selling the book, he would wear this costume and carry a tomahawk and musket. Sometimes he would smoke a peace pipe, perform a supposed war dance or whoop in a way that was apparently similar to the noises made by the Native Americans. During this time, he was given the nickname 'Indian Peter'. His unorthodox marketing methods appear to have worked: he sold 1,750 copies in York and Newcastle alone, making more than £30.[42]

He travelled around the country selling his book and eventually reached Aberdeen in 1758, hoping to reunite with his long-lost family. When he got there, he was arrested, jailed and charged with uttering 'a scurrilous and infamous libel on the corporation and city of Aberdeen'. The

---

[41] Equivalent to £40 nowadays.
[42] Equivalent to about £4,000 nowadays.

kidnappers had not taken kindly to Peter's description of their trade in children.

Peter knew that his only chance of being freed was by denying what he had written and saying that he had lied about Aberdeen's kidnapping trade. He was fined 10 shillings and banished from the city. The public hangman tore out the pages of his book which included Peter's accusations, then burned them at the Mercat Cross.

Peter travelled to Edinburgh, where some lawyers took up his case. The Court of Session ultimately rewarded him £180 for his unlawful arrest and imprisonment and £305 for his original kidnapping.[43] Finally, it appeared that there was a happy ending for Peter.

He settled in Edinburgh, got married, started a family but later divorced. Peter's entrepreneurial spirit came to the fore once again and he never missed an opportunity to make money. He invented a reaping machine for harvesting crops, published Edinburgh's first street directory and printed a weekly newspaper. Peter also opened a tavern and a coffee house. He also continued to capitalise on his Indian Peter persona by displaying a wooden figure of himself in his Native American outfit outside the tavern. The pub was particularly popular with the lawyers and judges of Edinburgh who would often retire there for dinner after an execution. It was remembered in a poem by Robert Fergusson, a young Scots writer who would be a great inspiration to Robert Burns. Peter also wrote several more books.

Most brilliantly, he started the city's first penny post, which enabled people to have their letters delivered anywhere in the city by a uniformed postman. It was not as successful a venture as he hoped so to make the business look like it was booming, he put numbers on the uniforms of his four employees: 1, 4, 8 and 16. His hope was that the people of Edinburgh would see these numbers and think he

---

[43] In total, equivalent to around £67,000 nowadays.

had far more employees than he actually had. It was a move typical of Indian Peter – always adroit at landing on his feet, turning a bad situation to his advantage and not averse to twisting the truth.

35. MARY HELEN YOUNG

Nazi-fighting Nurse

1883 - c. 1945

Standing at 4ft 11in, with white hair and a relentlessly cheerful demeanour, Mary Helen Young sounds more like a favourite granny than an active member of the French Resistance. But this ever-resilient nurse ended up dying in a concentration camp for her part in opposing the Nazi regime.

Mary Helen was born in Aberdeen and lost her mother while still a baby. Her father moved the family to Edinburgh and as a young woman, Mary Helen worked as a dressmaker at Jenners Department Store for several years. But she left that to train as a nurse in Surrey and, after qualifying, she moved to France in 1909, where she worked as a private nurse.

On the outbreak of the First World War, she was one of the first nurses in Paris to volunteer to serve with the Allied forces. Her work as a British Red Cross nurse during the war brought her close to the front line and one time she experienced 'a touch of gas', as the *Aberdeen Press and Journal* put it. This gassing would go on to have a negative impact on her health for the rest of her life.

She lost her fiancé in the war and decided to remain in Paris after its conclusion. She made trips every few years back to Aberdeen and Ballater to visit her sister and aunt respectively and even discussed setting up house with her sister, Elizabeth. When war broke out, Elizabeth 'was half-expecting' her sister to return home.

Mary Helen – who adopted the French form of her name, Marie Helene – instead chose to continue working in

Paris, even after the German occupation in June 1940. In December, she was sent to a civilian internment camp in eastern France. Due to poor health, she was released after six months and allowed to return home. From then on, Elizabeth got no news of her sister's whereabouts, only brief messages assuring her that all was well. Mary Helen, meanwhile, had taken a very dangerous step: she had joined the French Resistance.

Her house became a base for British agents who had gone to France to organise the Resistance. Secret radio messages were sent from her home to London. If that was not enough, Mary Helen also helped British airmen to escape the country.

This could not go on forever. Since her release from the camp, Mary Helen had been under Gestapo surveillance. In November 1943, she was arrested and interrogated. According to her friend in Ravensbruck concentration camp, Simone Saint-Clair, Mary Helen arrived at the camp in February 1944 'when the Germans could get nothing out of her'. In an interview with the *Aberdeen Press and Journal*, Saint-Clair described the awful conditions at Ravensbruck where the inmates were mostly female political prisoners and children. She described the forced labour, the typhoid and dysentery which were ever-present in the camp, and the rats that gnawed the fingers and toes of the babies during the night.

By this point, Mary Helen was 60 years old and in ill health. In a note passed to her sister through the Red Cross, she described her exhaustion and bad heart, possibly made worse by her gassing during the First World War. Investigations after the Second World War revealed that she was probably held in the concentration camp for about 12 months and that she may have died in a gas chamber, sometime in February or March 1945. Elizabeth did not learn that her sister was in a concentration camp or likely dead until after the war was over.

At a Court of Session hearing in Edinburgh in January 1948, which decided that Mary Helen must be presumed dead, the court heard numerous letters which testified to her courage and cheerfulness in the camp. Saint-Clair said: 'I know she would have died as she had lived, a brave Scotswoman. Right up to the very end, nothing could break her. She could smile, even in this hell the Germans had made for us. She was a brave woman, the bravest of the brave.'

36. PETER YOUNG

A Thief who Could Escape from Anywhere

c. 1764 - 1788

In autumn 1787, Peter Young was found guilty of shop-breaking and theft and was sentenced to be hanged in Aberdeen. As his execution was not to take place until November, special precautions were taken. Peter was kept in a cell by himself in the Tolbooth and no one was allowed in to see him unless accompanied by the jailer. Special handcuffs were made extra narrow for his small hands, and his legs were manacled to the 'lang gad', a long iron bar attached to the cell floor.

Why so many security measures just to lock up a thief? Peter had earned something of a reputation for his talents as an escape artist. He was said to have broken out of every prison in Scotland and that the prison cell which could hold him had yet to be built.

Peter's upbringing had certainly prepared him for such a life. Born in Mergie, near Stonehaven, his family were 'cairds' – an 18th-century term for travellers – and they made a living through low-level criminal activity. They were also well-connected in their community; his uncle was Charles 'Gle'ed' Graham, King of the Scottish Gypsies. Peter had an unconventional education. He never learned to read or write but did learn how to steal, pick locks and cut through iron bars. His small, gifted hands were perfect for making things, particularly saw knives.

By the time he was 18, he had been a soldier on both sides of the American War of Independence, a seaman in the British Navy and had escaped from prisons in both America and the Netherlands. To escape from the fortress in the Netherlands, he climbed an 18-foot wall using knotted-together blankets and then swam across a moat. He returned to Scotland with nothing worse to show from all these adventures than a scar on his temple.

On his return, he joined his uncle and his gang. Among them was Jean Wilson, his uncle's niece by marriage. She was an expert pickpocket, and she and Peter soon became common-law husband and wife.

Jean and Peter travelled to the North East of Scotland, accompanied by Agnes Brown, who was Jean's aunt and Peter's uncle's wife. They would target markets and crowds, sometimes getting their accomplices to stage a fight to distract members of the public. They would then move through the crowd, picking pockets. Peter and his wife were arrested more than 20 times but there was not enough evidence to prosecute them. Even when the authorities had proof, Peter escaped. Perhaps his most impressive getaway was from the thief's hole at Charlestown of Aboyne where he jumped over the heads of the crowd from the top outer steps of the hole.

Their luck ran out when they decided to target the crowds at a hanging in Aberdeen in 1787. Jean's aunt was arrested, flogged through the streets and sentenced to seven years in Australia. Peter and Jean fled to Banffshire where they were eventually captured and brought to Aberdeen to stand trial.

Both were sentenced to be executed. As Jean was pregnant, her sentence was deferred to August of the following year, after the baby's birth. Peter was condemned to die that November.

The night of his sentencing, a chinking sound was heard coming from Peter's cell. The place was searched and they found saw knives hidden in his chimney. After this incident, Peter seemed resigned to his fate and asked to see a minister to prepare him for death. He said to the head jailer: 'Aye, aye, Mister Gray. I winna come oot now till I come oot at the door.'

The jailer thought this meant Peter would only leave the Tolbooth when he went to his death on the gallows, but Peter had different ideas. Because Peter now seemed to focus his attention on the afterlife, he got permission to have three other prisoners visit him and read him the Bible. Under this pretence, Peter taught them lockpicking. They freed him from his handcuffs and cut the rivets on his leg irons, although he kept wearing them so the jailers would suspect nothing. They sawed through a window bar and disguised the cut with grease and rust.

At 8pm on 24 October, Peter and his accomplices made their move. They picked locks and forced their way through doors and an iron gate. They freed Peter's wife and her aunt as well as three other prisoners. At 3 o'clock in the morning, they took advantage of the changing of the guard and all nine of them walked out of the front door of the Tolbooth. It was exactly as Peter had promised Mr Gray: he came oot at the door.

They headed for the Laurencekirk area. One of the other prisoners was unwell and Peter carried him on his back for several miles. They sought shelter at the home of a man who was known to be a friend to criminals. The local laird and his men surrounded the house, with Peter once again escaping through a back window. However, his wife and her aunt were captured and sent back to the Aberdeen Tolbooth.

For a while, Peter roamed around Angus. In December, he teamed up with his uncle, Charles Graham. They were going to head back to Aberdeen and break out their wives. On their way north, they committed two burglaries in Arbroath. They were arrested and on New Year's Day 1788, Peter was transported to Aberdeen. His arms and legs were pinioned and he was accompanied by soldiers the whole way.

This time there were yet more security measures on the Aberdeen Tolbooth. The cut bars had been replaced and the flagstones in the cells were checked. When Peter arrived, he was strip-searched and kept in solitary confinement.

But still he kept trying. A jug of broth was delivered to him with six files hidden inside. Before he could use them, a message arrived from Edinburgh. The authorities had decided that the only place that could contain him was the Edinburgh Tolbooth.

When Peter arrived in Edinburgh, he was immediately chained to the lang gad by his leg irons. Less than an hour later, they found him sawing through his chains. He was searched and they found two more saw knives in his shoe.

Peter had one trick left up his sleeve. At his trial in March, he claimed it was all a case of mistaken identity and that he was not the man who had been sentenced in Aberdeen. It might have worked if it had not been for one thing: the distinctive scar on his temple marked him as the one and only Peter Young.

He was sentenced to die in July. A special cage made of plate iron was constructed for him inside his prison cell. The Edinburgh Tolbooth jailers were determined that he was not going to escape on their watch.

Six days before his execution, Peter resigned himself to his fate. He sent a lock of hair to his wife and dictated a letter for her. He left her instructions about their child and finished with these lines: 'My dear, what could a man do more than lay down his life to save his wife's? For in coming to save yours I lost my own.'

The day he was hanged, Jean gave birth to a baby girl. Peter was 24 years old.

ACKNOWLEDGEMENTS

This book is but a summary of what other, 'proper', researchers have found out before. I would not have been able to write it if it had not been for the efforts of individual historians who have spent hours doing the difficult leg work.

My thanks go to the staff at Aberdeen Central Library. Without the excellent resources provided by libraries, books like this one would be far harder to write and far more incomplete.

Thanks for the on-going support to my mum, Anne-Michelle Slater, who did not know I was writing a book, and my brother, Tomas Slater, who did.

Thanks to Sean Douglass whose conscientious editing has cut and polished this book till it shone. Any mistakes are, of course, not mine but his.

Thanks to Konain Ehsan who suffered through numerous bios and rewrites. His honesty and general lack of interest in Aberdonian history have been invaluable.

More generally, thanks to everyone who has supported or been a part of Scot Free Tours in the last three years.

Thanks to my grandfather Moray Slater for his endless supply of Aberdeen books, his support with double entry bookkeeping and his ceaseless encouragement of my business enterprise.

Thanks to Rick Meeken for bringing so much that is new (or new-old in the case of fresh stories) and good to Scot Free Tours.

Thanks to Melissa Geere and Nicola Marshall for being relentlessly interested in every new permutation and development and supporting me throughout all of them.

Finally, thanks to so many others who promoted the tours or fed me new stories or encouraged me to stick with it. And to those people without whom Scot Free Tours would never have existed – the tourees who turned up on a rainy Saturday morning, especially those who dragged along friends and family on further tours. Your support and enthusiasm are what has kept me going for so long. Thank you.

THEMATIC CONTENTS

TO BOLDLY GO
Travellers, explorers and pioneers
3. Thomas Blake Glover, 22. Dr Alexander Macklin, 25.
James Marr, 30. Mary Slessor

BATTLES ON DIFFERENT FRONTS
Men and women of war

10. George Findlater, 19. Professor R. V. Jones, 23. Rachel
Workman MacRobert, Lady MacRobert, 26. Dr Hugh
Mercer, 35. Mary Helen Young

INVENTIVE VISIONARIES
Creativity comes in many forms

2. Elizabeth Blackwell, 6. George Gordon Byron, 6th Baron
Byron, 14. Bill Gibb, 27. Lorna Moon, 29. John Reith,
1st Baron Reith, 33. David Welch

WILDCARDS
Defying categorisation

5. James Burnett, Lord Monboddo, 7. Alexander Cruden,
8. Sir Cosmo Duff-Gordon, 5th Baronet of Halkin, 11. Sir
Ewan Forbes, 11th Baronet of Craigievar, 34. Peter
Williamson

SELECTED BIBLIOGRAPHY

Oxford Dictionary of National Biography (online ed.). Oxford University Press.

J.H. ANDERSON

Bayer, Constance Pole, *The Great Wizard of the North, John Henry Anderson* (Watertown: R. Goulet's Magic Art Book Co., 1990)

ELIZABETH AND ALEXANDER BLACKWELL

Dictionary of National Biography, 1885 – 1900, Vol. 5 (London: Smith, Elder & Co, 1885)

Berg, Jo and Lagercrantz, Bo, *Scots in Sweden* (Stockholm: The Nordiska Musset The Swedish Institute, 1962)

Chambers, Thomas and Napier Thomson, Thomas, *A Biographical Dictionary of Eminent Scotsmen* (London: Blackie and Son, 1857)

THOMAS BLAKE GLOVER

Gardiner, Michael, *At the edge of empire: the life of Thomas Blake Glover* (Edinburgh: Birlinn, 2007)

WALFORD BODIE

Clark, David Finlay, *Chancer!: and other whimsical histories (*Aberdeen: Leopard, 2008)

Lead, Brian and Woods, Roger, *SHOWMEN OR CHARLATANS? The Stories of 'Dr' Walford Bodie and 'Sir' Alexander Cannon* (Published by the authors,

2003) https://www.lybrary.com/showmen-or-charlatans-the-stories-of-dr-walford-bodie-and-sir-alexander-cannon-p-289961.html

Newton, Andrew, 'The Electric Wizard – The Amazing Story of Dr Walford Bodie' *Newton Hypnosis* https://www.newtonhypnosis.com/electric-wizard-amazing-story-dr-walford-bodie/ [accessed 3/4/19]

JAMES BURNETT, LORD MONBODDO

Knight, William Angus, *Lord Monboddo and Some of His Contemporaries* (London: J. Murray, 1900)

MacDiarmid, Hugh, *Scottish Eccentrics* (Manchester: Carcanet [in association with] Mid Northumberland Arts Group, 1993.)

GEORGE GORDON BYRON, 6TH BARON BYRON

Rogerson, W., *Lord Byron's connection with Aberdeen*, (Aberdeen: Bon Accord, 1902)

ALEXANDER CRUDEN

Keay, Julia, *Alexander Cruden: The Tormented Genius Who Unwrote the Bible* (London: HarperCollins, 2004)

DONALD DINNIE

Webster, David Pirie, *Donald Dinnie: The First Sporting Superstar* (Buchan: Ardo Publishing, 1999)

SIR COSMO DUFF-GORDON, 5TH BARONET OF HALKIN

'British Wreck Commissioner's Inquiry: Day 10 Testimony of Sir Cosmo Duff-

Gordon' https://www.titanicinquiry.org/BOTInq/BOTIn q10Duff-Gordon01.php

Encyclopedia Titanica https://www.encyclopedia-titanica.org/ [accessed 22.1.19]

Grice, Elizabeth, 'Titanic Survivors Vindicated at Last', *The Telegraph* 13.4.12 https://www.telegraph.co.uk/history/tita nic-anniversary/9202821/Titanic-survivors-vindicated-at-last.html

GEORGE FINDLATER

Cross, Craig, 'Piper Findlater VC: Hero of Dargai' *Craig Cross* http://www.craigcross.co.uk/History/Findlater/Cha pter1.html [accessed 4.3.19]

SIR EWAN FORBES, 11TH BARONET
OF CRAIGIEVAR, AND WILLIAM FORBES-
SEMPILL, 19TH LORD SEMPILL

Barnes, Lesley-Ann, 'Gender Identity and Scottish Law: the Legal Response to Transsexuality' *Edinburgh Law Review* 11.2 pp. 162-186

Lashmar, Paul and Mullins, Andrew, 'Churchill protected Scottish peer suspected of spying for Japan' *The Independent* 24.8.98 https://www.independent.co.uk/news/ churchill-protected-scottish-peer-suspected-of-spying-for-japan-1173730.html

MARY GARDEN

Turnbull, Michael, *Mary Garden* (Aldershot: Scolar Press, 1997)

SHEILA AND MAXWELL GARVIE

Garvie, Sheila, *Marriage to Murder* (Edinburgh: Chambers, 1980)

'Why we murdered a millionaire; For the first time, Brian Tevendale reveals how he and Sheila Garvie plotted to kill her rich but brutal husband Max' <u>The Free Library</u>. 1999 *Scottish* *Daily Record* https://www.thefreelibrary.com/Why+we+murder ed+a+millionaire%3b+For+the+first+time%2c+Brian+T evendale...-a060432932 [accessed 4.6.19]

'The Sins of My Mother' *The Scotsman* 1.2.02 https://www.scotsman.com/lifestyle-2-15039/the-sins-of-my-mother-1-595767 [accessed 4.6.19]

BILL GIBB

Rew, Christine, *Bill Gibb: The Golden Boy of British Fashion* (Aberdeen: Aberdeen City Council, 2003)

Webb, Iain R, *Bill Gibb: Fashion and Fantasy* (London: V&A, 2008)

DR ALEXANDER GORDON

Smith, Lesley, 'Dr Alexander Gordon of Aberdeen' *J Fam Plann Reprod Health Care* 2010 36: 253

Dunn, Peter M 'Dr Alexander Gordon (1752-99) and contagious puerperal fever' *Archives of Disease in Childhood - Fetal and Neonatal Edition* 1998;78: F232-F233.

Burch, Druin, 'When Childbirth Was Natural, and Deadly' *Live Science* 10.1.09 https://www.livescience.com/3210-childbirth-natural-deadly.html

JANE, DUCHESS OF GORDON

Graham, Harry, *A Group of Scottish Women* (New York: Duffield & Co., 1908)

ISHBEL HAMILTON-GORDON, LADY ABERDEEN

French, Doris, *Ishbel And The Empire: A Biography of Lady Aberdeen* (Toronto: Dundurn, 1988)

DR ROBERT HENDERSON

Moore, Charles, *Margaret Thatcher: The Authorized Biography. Volume One: Not For Turning* (London: Allen Lane, 2013)

PROFESSOR R. V. JONES

Churchill, Winston S. Sir, *Second World War Vol 2: Their Finest Hour* (London: Cassell & Co., 1955)

Jones, R. V., *Most Secret War* (London: Penguin, 2009)

DR ROBERT DANIEL LAWRENCE

Lawrence, Jane, *Diabetes, Insulin and the life of R. D. Lawrence* (London: Royal Society of Medicine Press, 2012)

ISABELLA MACDUFF, COUNTESS OF BUCHAN

Cornell, David, *Bannockburn: The Triumph of Robert the Bruce* (New Haven: Yale University Press, 2009)

ALEXANDER MACKLIN

Lansing, Alfred, *Endurance* (London: Weidenfeld & Nicolson, 2002)

Wild, Frank, The Story of the Quest (London: Cassell & Co., 1923)

RACHEL WORKMAN MACROBERT, LADY MACROBERT

Miller, Marion, *Cawnpore to Cromar: the MacRoberts of Douneside* (Kinloss: Librario, 2014)

SIR PATRICK MANSON

Manson-Bahr, Philip Henry Sir, *Patrick Manson, the father of tropical medicine* (London, New York: T. Nelson 1962)

JAMES MARR

Haddelsey, Stephen, *Operation Tabarin: Britain's secret wartime expedition to Antarctica, 1944-46* (Stroud, Gloucestershire: The History Press, 2014)

HUGH MERCER

Horne, Tom, 'What the Internet Taught Me About Hugh Mercer' *Love Archaeology Magazine* 31.1.15 https://www.academia.edu/10707233/Blog_What_The_Internet_Taught_Me_About_Hugh_Mercer [accessed 4.6.19]

Felder, Paula S. 'Hugh Mercer: An Unexpected Life' *The Free Lance-Star* 9.4.04 https://web.archive.org/web/20050516210156/http://www.freelancestar.com/News/FLS/2004/092004/09042004/1488210 [accessed 4.6.19]

LORNA MOON

De Mille, Richard, *My Secret Mother, Lorna Moon* (New York: Farrar, Straus & Giroux, 1998)

Moon, Lorna, *The collected works of Lorna Moon* (Edinburgh: Black & White, 2002)

JOHNNY RAMENSKY

Jeffery, Robert, *Gentle Johnny Ramensky: the extraordinary true story of the safe blower who became a war hero* (Edinburgh: Black & White, 2011)

JOHN REITH, 1ST BARON REITH

'History of the BBC: John Reith' *BBC* https://www.bbc.co.uk/historyofthebbc/research/culture/reith-1 [accessed 4.6.19]

MARY SLESSOR

Buchan, James, *The expendable Mary Slessor* (Edinburgh: St Andrew Press, 1980)

Robertson, Elizabeth, *Mary Slessor* (Edinburgh: National Museums of Scotland, 2000)

ALEXANDER STEWART, EARL OF MAR

Brown, Michael, 'Regional Lordship in North-East Scotland: The Badenoch Stewarts, II. Alexander Stewart Earl of Mar' *Northern Scotland*, Volume 16 (First Series) Issue 1, pp31-53

Crawfurd, George, *A General Description of the Shire of Renfrew* (Paisley: J. Neilson, 1818)

McMenemy, Elma, *Bloody Scottish History: Aberdeen* (Stroud: The History Press, 2014)

MARY ANN SUTHERLAND AKA MRS GORDON BAILLIE

Archibald, Malcolm, *Fishermen, Randies and Fraudsters* (Edinburgh: B&W, 2014)

DAVID WELCH

'David Welch' *The Herald* 23.9.2000 https://www.heraldscotland.com/news/12157304.david-welch/ [accessed 4.6.19]

'David Welch' *The Telegraph* 21.9.2000 https://www.telegraph.co.uk/news/obituaries/1356156/David-Welch.html [accessed 4.6.19]

PETER WILLIAMSON

Skelton, Douglas, *Indian Peter: the Extraordinary Life and Adventures of Peter Williamson* (Edinburgh: Mainstream, 2005)

MARY HELEN YOUNG

'Nazis sent Aberdeen Heroine to Gas Chamber' *Aberdeen Press and Journal* 27.9.1945 https://www.britishnewspaperarchive.co.uk/viewer/bl/0000578/19450927/002/0001 [accessed 9.4.19]

'Gallant Nurse aided underground work' *Aberdeen Press and Journal* 28.9.1945 https://www.britishnewspaperarchive.co.uk/viewer/bl/0000578/19450928/040/0004 [accessed 9.4.19]

'Nazis Murdered Nurse for Aiding French' *Aberdeen Press and Journal* 31.1.1948 https://www.britishnewspaperarchive.co.uk/viewer/bl/0000578/19480131/074/0006 [accessed 9.4.19]

PETER YOUNG

Adams, Norman, *Hangman's Brae: True Crime and Punishment in Aberdeen and the North-East* (Edinburgh: Black & White, 2005)

UNUSUAL ABERDONIANS

.

ABOUT THE AUTHOR

Lia Sanders

Lia has been guiding tours for more than five years, firstly in Edinburgh and then in her hometown of Aberdeen. As well as tours of the streets of Aberdeen, she has done tours of the Maritime Museum and nearby Dunnottar Castle. In 2016, she set up Scot Free Tours to challenge people's perceptions of Aberdeen by telling them lesser-known stories of the city. Scot Free Tours is now the top-ranked tour provider in Aberdeen, collecting TripAdvisor Certificates of Excellence in 2018 and 2019.

On her tours, Lia focuses on the stories of individuals, preferably the funny, gruesome or unexpected bits. These are the tales that she hopes will come to life for you as you read this book.